CAMBRIDGE STUDIES IN PHILOSOPHY

A Combinatorial theory of possibility

CAMBRIDGE STUDIES IN PHILOSOPHY

General editor SYDNEY SHOEMAKER

Advisory editors J. E. J. ALTHAM, SIMON BLACKBURN,
GILBERT HARMAN, MARTIN HOLLIS, FRANK JACKSON
JONATHAN LEAR, WILLIAM LYCAN, JOHN PERRY, BARRY STROUD

A Combinatorial theory of possibility

D. M. Armstrong

Challis Professor of Philosophy
University of Sydney

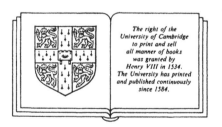

The right of the
University of Cambridge
to print and sell
all manner of books
was granted by
Henry VIII in 1534.
The University has printed
and published continuously
since 1584.

Cambridge University Press

Cambridge
New York   Port Chester   Melbourne   Sydney

CAMBRIDGE UNIVERSITY PRESS
Cambridge, New York, Melbourne, Madrid, Cape Town, Singapore, São Paulo

Cambridge University Press
The Edinburgh Building, Cambridge CB2 8RU, UK

Published in the United States of America by Cambridge University Press, New York

www.cambridge.org
Information on this title: www.cambridge.org/9780521374279

© Cambridge University Press 1989

This publication is in copyright. Subject to statutory exception
and to the provisions of relevant collective licensing agreements,
no reproduction of any part may take place without the written
permission of Cambridge University Press.

First published 1989

A catalogue record for this publication is available from the British Library

Library of Congress Cataloguing in Publication data

Amstrong, D. M. (David Malet), 1926–
A Combinatorial theory of possibility / D.M. Armstrong.
p.   cm. – (Cambridge studies in philosophy)
Includes index.
ISBN 0-521-37427-8. – ISBN 0-521-37780-3 (pbk.)
1. Possibility. 2. Logical atomism. I. Title. II. Series.
BC199.P7A76   1989
146′ .5 – dc19
89–708
CIP

ISBN 978-0-521-37427-9 hardback
ISBN 978-0-521-37780-5 paperback

Transferred to digital printing 2007

For Elizabeth

Contents

vii

Preface

What is put forward in this essay is a new version of the metaphysic of *Logical Atomism*. It is a Logical Atomism completely purged of *semantic* and *epistemic* atomism. The idea that one can reach the atoms by analysing meanings is utterly rejected. In general, it is not for philosophers to say what the fundamental constituents of the world are. That question is to be settled *a posteriori*. It is a question for total science.

The version of Logical Atomism put forward here even abstracts from the question of whether there are any atoms at all at the bottom of the world. That too is a question to be decided *a posteriori*, if it can be decided at all. In Chapter 5 I argue that Logical Atomism can still be sustained even if we never get past merely relative atoms.

But if there may be no genuine atoms, why continue to speak of Logical Atomism? I do so because, with a little qualification, the scheme presented cleaves to the fundamental idea that the states of affairs into which the world divides (Wittgenstein's and Russell's *atomic facts*) are logically independent of each other. Each one is, as I will say, 'Hume distinct' from every other.

This becomes the basis of what I think is a simple (and naturalistic) Combinatorial theory of possibility. In his article 'Tractarian Nominalism' Brian Skyrms sketches a metaphysics of facts (states of affairs, as I put it), facts having as constituents individuals and universals (the latter divided into properties and relations). I had already argued for such a position in my book *Universals and Scientific Realism* (1978a, b). What I had not noticed was what Skyrms pointed out: that this could become the basis for a theory of possibility. The present work is an attempt to develop Skyrms's insight. With his approval, and the permission of the D. Reidel Publishing Company, his article is reprinted at the end of this volume as an appendix.

I spoke just now of a qualification of my Logical Atomism. The qualification is needed because, agreeing with Russell and disagreeing with Skyrms, I do not think the world is one consisting solely of *first-order* states of affairs. We require in addition *at least* one higher-order state of affairs, namely, the fact that the conjunction of all the lower-order states of affairs *is* all the lower-order states of affairs. Russell called this a 'general fact'. This state of affairs, however, is not Hume independent of the lower-order states of affairs. It is true that it is contingent that a certain conjunction of states of affairs is the totality of lower-order states of affairs. But the general fact is a fact about just that conjunction. (It is, I shall argue, a dyadic relation having that conjunction as one term.) As a result, it necessitates the existence of that conjunction, and so the *two*-way logical independence required for Hume independence is not achieved.

This failure of Hume independence seems relatively trivial. Indeed, a similar phenomenon is already present with first-order states of affairs. The existence of *a*, R and *b* by no means necessitates that *a* has R to *b*. But if *a* has R to *b*, then *a*, R and *b* must exist.

I do not think, however, that general facts – states of affairs of totality, as I call them – exhaust the higher-order states of affairs. Many analytic philosophers still cripple themselves with the heavy burden of a sceptical or Regularity theory of causation and law. It is Hume's fatal legacy. (I criticized the Regularity theory of *law* at some length in my 1983 book.) To rescue ourselves from such a theory of law it seems necessary to postulate higher-order states of affairs: relations between universals and also, I think, properties of universals, the latter required for functional laws. The lower-order states of affairs never necessitate any higher-order states of affairs, but, for example, a relation of necessitation between universals does necessitate a first-order regularity (though with a qualification that will be noted later). This necessitation, however, has seemed far from trivial to many commentators. Rather, they say, it is a logical link involving mystery and magic.

I believe that this is not in fact the case. A relation of necessitation between universals may be understood thus: A certain *sort* of state of affairs ensures that a further state of affairs of a certain *sort* exists, a further state of affairs having a certain relation to the first state of affairs (e.g. involving the same particular). Provided that we understand what *ensuring* is, the necessitation of a corresponding regularity would seem to be perspicuous enough. I think it is analytic.

And as for the notion of ensuring, Humean prejudices about its analysis aside it is one that we are given in direct experience, in particular cases at least (pressure on our own body being the most salient case).

The theory of states of affairs (facts) is, of course, central to a Logical Atomism. I developed a theory of states of affairs in my book on universals. States of affairs, I said, involve both particulars and universals, neither being found outside states of affairs. In the present work the theory is in some degree developed. In particular, occasion is taken to correct two errors.

First, I have come to realize that it is a necessary truth that the internal structure of universals is whatever it is. Previously I had taken it as a contingent matter whether, for instance, a certain property is simple or complex. But how could one and the same universal have different structures in different worlds? The question of the structure of a certain universal may well have to be decided, if it can be decided, *a posteriori*. But that does not make the matter a contingent one. The influence of Kripke will be obvious here, although I reject some of his other alleged necessities discovered *a posteriori* (e.g. necessities of origin).

Second, I now think that the relation of a complex universal to its constituents cannot be assimilated to a *mereological* relation. Although the universal P, for instance, is a constituent of the conjunctive universal *P&Q*, it is not a mereological part of that complex universal. The reason for this, to be spelt out in the main text, is that complex universals embed states of affairs, and states of affairs have a non-mereological mode of composition.

My understanding of the point that constituent universals are not mereological parts of the complex universals of which they are constituents is due to David Lewis. Not that he accepts states of affairs into his ontology. For him, worlds are worlds of things, not of facts. But as Nietzsche said, from a good opponent one draws strength. One draws all the more strength when that opponent is continuously concerned that his adversary's position should be developed as rigorously and plausibly as possible. Lewis has been so kind as to criticize two drafts of this book in a consistently helpful way. He has saved me from many errors.

In Chapter 6, Section II, there is some discussion of *quantity*. The context is the difficulty for a Combinatorial theory of possibility posed by the fact that different determinates falling under the same determinable cannot qualify the one individual at one time. Ideally, what is required is a fully worked-out theory of what quantities are: an extension of the theory of universals to cover quantities. Chris Swoyer's paper 'The Metaphysics of Measurement' (1987), which construes a quantity as a class of properties, seems largely to fill the gap. A paper by John Bigelow and Robert Pargetter, 'Quantities' (1988), construed quantities as classes of universals, but relations rather than properties. I criticized Bigelow and Pargetter, and returned to Swoyer's view, in a paper entitled 'Are Quantities Relations?' (1988).

No Logical Atomism can be complete without some treatment of mathematical entities and truths. These topics are taken up in Chapter 9. Building on work by Forrest and Armstrong (1987), and resurrecting an old idea, I argue that numbers (natural, rational and real) are all relations of proportion, relations which are internal to their terms. As a result, they do not appear in the logically independent states of affairs that go to make up possible worlds. I argue that mathematical truths are necessary, known *a priori* if they are known, and analytic. I take the occasion to offer a theory of *sets*. They are identified with certain conjunctive states of affairs, where the constituent states of affairs involve the members of the set in question.

In 1985 I presented a paper, 'The Nature of Possibility', which stated some of the central themes of the present essay, at the Chapel Hill symposium in North Carolina. The paper was published in the *Canadian Journal of Philosophy* in 1986, together with an excellent commentary and criticism by Jaegwon Kim, originally delivered at the symposium. Since then there has been a paper by Ray Bradley – 'Possibility and Combinatorialism: Wittgenstein Versus Armstrong' (1989). Bradley contests my interpretation of Wittgenstein, a topic about which I make no claim to expertise.

As already acknowledged, my principal intellectual debt in writing this book is to David Lewis. Much of the material was presented to a seminar I gave at the University of Wisconsin in Madison in the fall of 1985. Helpful discussion and criticism came from many people, including Fred Dretske, Berent Enç, Scott Shalkowski and Elliot Sober. Members of my fourth-year/postgraduate seminar at Sydney in 1986 and 1987 – Rodney Rutherford and Peter Godfrey-

Smith in particular – gave me much to think about. I have had other useful comments from John Bigelow, Peter Forrest, Bill Lycan, Graham Oddie, Brian Skyrms, Michael Tooley and the anonymous referee for Cambridge University Press. I am greatly indebted to Anthea Bankoff for the typing of successive drafts.

PART I

Non-Naturalist theories of possibility

1

The causal argument

I THEORIES OF POSSIBILITY

Every systematic philosophy must give some account of the nature of possibility. The main constraint I wish to place on such an account is that it be compatible with *Naturalism*. The term 'Naturalism' is often used rather vaguely, but I shall understand by it the doctrine that nothing at all exists except the single world of space and time. So my objective is to give an account of possibility which is in no way other-worldly.

A non-Naturalist theory of possibility tries to account for the notion by postulating entities additional to the world of space and time, for instance, possible worlds or 'abstract' propositions. It will be useful to begin by criticizing some non-Naturalist theories, concentrating especially on the account given by David Lewis.

Among the non-Naturalist theories of possibility there is one, not Lewis's, which has a central place. This is because other theories can be seen as reactions to it. The theory is popularly attributed to Leibniz, although the textual warrant for this is dubious. But it is convenient to call it the Leibnizian view.

According to this view, over and above the actual world there are an indefinite multiplicity of merely possible worlds. They constitute all the ways that the world could have been. Included in the actual world are its past, its present and its future. The actual world contains minds, perhaps matter, perhaps God, perhaps still stranger things. The actual world is a possible world. The *other* possible worlds, the merely possible worlds, are ways that the actual world might have been.

A contingent truth is, then, defined as a truth true in the actual world but false in some possible world. A contingent falsehood is false in the actual world but true in some possible world. A necessary truth is true in all possible worlds; a necessary falsehood is false in all possible worlds.

Contingent truths, contingent falsities and necessary truths all

3

state possibilities. But *contingent falsities* give us the central cases of possibility, the cases for which the concept of possibility was introduced.

It is natural to develop this view by saying that it involves *two levels of being*. The actual world has the superior sort of being: actuality. The merely possible worlds have some sort of being, but they lack actuality.

I have just said that this view occupies a central place among non-Naturalist theories of possibility. But I do not mean that it is widely adopted. Many philosophers reject the notion of levels of being. Furthermore, as we shall see, there is a very powerful epistemological argument, due to D. C. Williams, which seems an almost conclusive objection to this view. The centrality of the Leibnizian view is constituted only by this: It is easy and natural to see other non-Naturalist theories as reacting to, and trying to mitigate, the difficulties of this view.

David Lewis (1986a) reacts by trying to *raise* the status of the merely possible worlds. His theory may be said to out-Leibniz Leibniz. Lewis advocates an *indexical* theory of actuality. Not only this world but every possible world is actual (from its own point of view). (Compare: 'Everybody is *I*, from that person's own point of view'.) Every possible world, *including this world*, is merely possible from the point of view of other worlds. (Compare: 'Everybody is *another* from the point of view of anybody else'.) In this way Lewis re-establishes egalitarianism among the possible worlds.

An examination of the strengths and weaknesses of Lewis's theory takes us deep into the theory of possibility. It will be discussed at length in the next chapter.

Both the Leibnizian theory and Lewis's theory postulate what one might call *genuine* possible worlds. (They are *realist* theories, with Lewis's the more thoroughgoing realism.) But there are accounts of possibility which try to give truth-conditions for statements of possibility, and for *talk* about possible worlds, but without really postulating possible worlds. Lewis calls such theories '*Ersatz*' theories ('Paradise on the cheap'). The theory to be defended in Part II is a form of *Ersatz* theory.[1] It gives an account of talk about possible worlds, and talk about possibility, in terms of

---

1 This statement will have to be qualified a little. Strictly, my view is a Fictionalist rather than an *Ersatz* view. See Chapter 3, Sections III and IV.

recombinations of elements found in the natural world. At this point, however, we are interested in *Ersatz* theories which appeal to entities *over and above those admitted by Naturalists*.

Non-Naturalists who hold *Ersatz* theories postulate certain *actual* entities over and above those entities postulated by Naturalists. They then try to construct substitutes for possible worlds, and to give an account of possibilities, with the aid of those non-Natural, but actual, entities.

Suppose, for instance, that one believes, as many philosophers have believed, that there are *objective propositions*. These propositions, one may think, are not spatio-temporal entities; they exist independently of any mind, and they can be true or not true. Such propositions then function as the objects of mental states such as belief. To believe that p is to stand in a certain sort of relation to the objective proposition p.

These propositions, part of actuality but not part of spatio-temporal reality, can then be used to build *Ersatz* possible worlds. Robert Adams (1974) does it this way. Consider a domain which contains every pair of mutually contradictory propositions. Sets can be formed which draw no more than one member from each such pair, and where the members of the set are all consistent with each other. The set is *maximally* consistent if and only if no further proposition can be drawn from further contradictory pairs without making the set inconsistent. Such a maximally consistent set is called *a world-story*.

Such world-stories are not *worlds*. For this is an Actualist theory, that is, one which, unlike Leibniz and Lewis, recognizes only one world. But the theory can provide truth-conditions for *talk* about possible worlds. Thus:

There is a possible world in which p

has as truth-condition:

The proposition that p is a member of some world-story.

Again,

In every possible world, q

has as truth-condition:

The proposition that q is a member of every world-story.

Non-Naturalist but Actualist theories of possibility may be developed in different ways, but for my purposes I think that

Adams's theory is a sufficient representative. We have a threefold classification. There are two Realisms about possible worlds: the Leibnizian and the Lewisian, the latter a completely full-blooded Realism. In the Leibnizian scheme only one world is actual; the others are merely possible. In Lewis's theory every world is actual from its own standpoint, but merely possible from the standpoint of every other world. Non-Naturalist Actualists agree with the Leibnizian view that there is only one actual world. But, unlike Leibniz, they deny that there are any merely possible worlds, except in a manner of speaking. At the same time, they hold that actuality goes beyond the Naturalist's world of space and time. These non-Natural entities are then appealed to in order to yield truth-conditions for *talk* about possible worlds and possibilities.

Lewis says that non-Naturalist Actualists want the paradise of possible worlds on the cheap. I hope to attain that paradise at a still cheaper rate. Having criticized the three types of non-Naturalist theory, I shall develop a Naturalist theory of possibility and possible worlds. It will subordinate possibility to actuality, and furthermore to an actuality modestly, naturalistically, conceived.

It is to be noted that all the theories to be considered involve versions of the notion of possible worlds. The heuristic value, at least, of using the notion of such worlds seems to have been amply demonstrated in recent philosophical work (see Lewis 1986a, Chapter 1). Here I will mention just one application of the notion, an application of special value in metaphysical investigation, an application that will be made at a number of points later in this essay. I have in mind the notion of *supervenience*.

Suppose that one considers a certain subset of worlds, where each member of the subset has certain features in common. For instance, suppose that in each such world, the individuals in that world are distributed according to the same pattern, having exactly the same properties and relations. It may appear a plausible claim that, in each such world, certain further, or ostensibly further, features are fixed. For instance, in the case just considered, it appears that the *resemblances* of all individuals do not differ from world to world. The resemblances are then *supervenient* on the original features, the pattern of qualities and relations, which each world had in common.

What conclusions may be drawn from superveniences thus defined? The conclusion I wish to draw, the conclusion that gives this notion of supervenience its special interest, is that the supervenient is not really a feature of the world distinct from the features it supervenes on. The resemblances of things, for instance, are not really distinct from the properties and relations of things. We seem to be able to add that the properties and relations of things *fail* to supervene on their mere resemblances. For a different set of properties and relations might have exactly the same resemblance-structure. If this addition is correct, then it seems that we have here an argument for taking properties and relations to be primary, resemblances to be secondary.

II THE CAUSAL ARGUMENT

I will now advance an argument intended as a difficulty for any non-Naturalist account of possibility. The premiss of the argument is that the objects postulated by non-Naturalist theories of possibility stand in no causal (or nomic) relation to the world of space and time. The conclusion is that we have no good reason to postulate such entities.

The premiss is conceded by non-Naturalists. Other possible worlds, whether Leibnizian or Lewisian, are not thought to have any effect on our actual world. Nor is there thought to be any non-causal law of nature linking such worlds with our world. In the case of non-Naturalist Actualism, the non-spatio-temporal propositions, or other entities from which the surrogates of possible worlds are constructed, do not even have causal or nomic relations to each other, much less causal or nomic relations to our space-time world.

I do not claim that this premiss gives us a *conclusive* reason for denying the existence of such entities. But I think it gives us a good reason for denying their existence. Our world of space and time is epistemically very secure. We have strong reasons indeed, derived both from bedrock common sense and natural science, to postulate its existence. (Even to use the word 'postulate' is to imply some lack of rational certainty, an implication which is potentially misleading.) To postulate entities which lie beyond our world of space and time is, in general, to make a speculative, uncertain, postulation. The postulation may perhaps be defended if it can be presented as *explaining* some or all of the spatio-temporal phenomena. But if the entities postulated lie beyond our world, and in addition have

7

no causal or nomic connection with it, then the postulation has no explanatory value. Hence (a further step, of course) we ought to deny the existence of such entities.

Non-natural *possibilia* are often defended by their upholders as theoretical postulations. Consider, therefore, the theoretical postulations of natural science. The explanatory value of the latter derives from the fact that the entity postulated makes a causal/nomic contribution to the natural world. No doubt it is wrong to say that every such postulated entity is a cause (or an effect). The postulated thing might be a *property*, and properties are not causes or effects. For instance, *positive electric charge* is neither cause nor effect. But objects can act causally in virtue of their positive electric charge, and that is the point of postulating such a property. The postulated thing might be a causal connection, or a law, either a causal law or a law of coexistence, and such connections are not causes or effects. But a causal/nomic connection obviously makes a causal/nomic contribution to the world.

By contrast, other possible worlds, or maximally consistent sets of immaterial propositions, are in no way causally or nomically linked to our world of space and time. They are postulated for purely *semantic* reasons. We appear to be able to make true statements involving possibilities and necessities. It is then argued that these statements demand truth-makers and that these truth-makers lie beyond our space-time world.

These semantic postulations, however, in no way explain anything that happens in the natural world. Hence there seems no reason to make them. I will illustrate the force of the argument by considering an analogous case.

Suppose that one was a Dualist in the philosophy of mind, and that one also held a Representative theory of perception. According to the latter theory, the immediate objects of sensory awareness are sense-data, or sense-impressions, which correspond, or fail to correspond, to physical states of affairs. But suppose in addition that one held the Representative theory in an eccentric form. Suppose that one held that the physical world stands in no causal or nomic relations to the succession of sense-data in individual minds.

Such a theorist might be asked what reason he thinks he has to postulate the existence of a physical world. Suppose that he answered that his reason was a semantic one. We continually make statements about physical objects and events. Such talk is in practice quite ineliminable. Moreover, we think that such statements are very often true. Furthermore, the statements, whether true or false, clearly purport to refer beyond sense-data, or any other content of our minds. Hence, this eccentric continues, we require physical objects, things quite other than sense-data, to serve as truth-makers for statements about sticks and stones, even though the latter are never causes of our perceptions.

I take it that it is clear that such a thinker would have put up a very weak case for the existence of physical objects *so conceived*. As a matter of fact, he would have a weak case even if he took the line that Malebranche took and postulated a God who was cause both of the order of our sense-data and of the physical order. Even with such an indirect causal link between minds and the physical world, the justification for postulating the latter would be very thin, as Berkeley saw clearly. But what of an atheistic Malebranche arguing for the existence of independently existing physical objects? His case would be desperate indeed.

I suggest that the case for possible worlds or other *possibilia* lying beyond our world of space and time is equally desperate.

Strong as this argument seems, there are two considerations which should perhaps give us pause. The first, and most powerful, may be termed the Objection from Mathematics. (Logic perhaps gives rise to similar objections, but here I will restrict myself to mathematics.) The objection may be introduced by remarking that if the argument against Non-Naturalist accounts of possibility has any force, then it should equally have force against many *other* entities postulated by some philosophers. An example would be the postulation of transcendent universals. This extension of the argument to such universals is to be welcomed, I think. It does not weaken the argument in any significant degree. For it is not as if transcendent universals have a high epistemic credit rating. With mathematics, however, the situation is quite different.

Mathematics has given us an immensely fruitful, and steadily growing, body of results. It is hard to doubt that we now have an enormous body of mathematical *knowledge*. Moreover, this body of knowledge is of the utmost value for physical investigations. Natural science would be almost nothing without it. The question then arises, for philosophers at least, what mathematics is *about*. What are the truth-makers for true mathematical statements? It has often been claimed that these truth-makers are not in space and time. If that is the true position, presumably they do not act on things in space and time. Upholders of non-Naturalistic theories of possibility can then shelter behind the skirts of mathematics. If mathematics requires non-natural entities, and, moreover, these entities have no effects upon nature, why should not theories of possibility postulate impotent non-natural entities in a similar way?

So an obligation on an upholder of the Causal argument will be to give an account of the truth of the propositions of mathematics without invoking non-spatio-temporal entities. Or, if the truth of mathematics is denied, as it has been recently by Hartry Field (1980), the obligation will be transformed into giving an account of the *efficacy* of mathematics in helping us to move from truths about the world of space and time to further truths about that world, without postulating non-spatio-temporal entities. The Causal argument itself gives us a strong intellectual motive for thinking that there is *some* satisfactory account of mathematics which is compatible with Naturalism. But without actually providing such an account of mathematics, the upholder of the Causal argument can hardly rest easy.

But, as David Lewis has pointed out in discussion, it is by no means sufficient for an upholder of the Causal argument to give a Naturalistic account of mathematics, if all that means is that mathematical entities are located in space and time. An opponent can argue *ad hominem* in the following way. What good will it do to drag mathematical entities down to earth if, when so dragged down, they remain causally impotent? If causally idle aspects of the natural world are countenanced, why not causally idle elements that lie beyond the natural world?

To illustrate the force of these two obligations on an upholder of the Causal argument in a more concrete way, let us consider the mathematical discipline of set theory. Set theory is peculiarly important here because mathematics can be exhibited as involving nothing but set-theoretical propositions about set-theoretical entities.

Apparently under the influence of Quine, it is customary to argue that set theory deals with Platonic objects. But Lewis has recently tentatively suggested (1986a, p. 83) that in the case of sets whose members are spatio-temporal entities, the sets are located wherever their members are located. The location is like the location of spatio-temporal aggregates, especially those cases where the

10

parts of the aggregate are scattered. Sets of such sets are to be similarly located.

If this is correct (and I shall not discuss here whether it is correct, although I sympathize with the suggestion), then a set theory limited to spatio-temporal objects does not challenge Naturalism. Such a limitation will give the Naturalist what he needs. He may have to deny that there is literally such an object as the *null class*. But that seems a negotiable degree of scepticism. (Even that turns out not to be necessary. See Chapter 9, Section IV.)

But has this move helped the upholder of the Causal argument? Sets are where their members are. But does that give them any more causal power than if they are other-worldly? Is it not the *members* of (first-order) sets which *act*?

What I think a supporter of the Causal argument can say in reply to this point is that it may be evaded provided that the apparently impotent entities are *supervenient* on entities which are in some way causally potent. The notion of supervenience, as I have already indicated (Chapter 1, Section I), is best defined by an appeal to the notion of possible worlds, and so cannot be discussed in any depth at this point. But it is essential to this defence of the Causal argument to maintain, as I do maintain, that what supervenes is not really distinct from what it supervenes on.

Now in the case of sets, it seems clear that they supervene on their members. Going down the hierarchy, they supervene on the members of the first-order sets, members of which are not sets. But if the sets are not really distinct from what they supervene on, then, provided the latter have causal powers, any causal impotence of the sets is either non-existent or a trivial phenomenon reflecting special features of the way we talk about sets.

So I suggest that the upholder of the Causal argument against other-worldly possibilities may reply to the Objection from Mathematics by arguing that the truth-makers for mathematics are either entities in nature with causal powers, or else that they supervene on such entities. The Causal argument itself may be used as a reason for upholding some such account of mathematics.

This reply is programmatic only. It requires to be supplemented by a positive account of mathematical entities and mathematical truth. Such an account will be attempted in Chapter 9. To this will be subjoined an account of the nature of sets.

I pass to a second consideration which may cast doubt on the

Causal argument. Does not natural science itself postulate entities which are causally and nomically inert? Consider, in particular, Newtonian absolute space and time. It does no more than provide a neutral backdrop for causally active matter.

I do not believe that this objection to the Causal argument is anywhere near as weighty as the Objection from Mathematics. The Newtonian conception of space and time is not favoured by current cosmology. Space-time which is empty of matter is allowed. But there is no portion of space-time which is not the locus of a field of force, at least. Hence, every portion of space-time may be thought of as causally active, or at least as having causal potential.

As a result, I suggest that we can without misgiving uphold the Causal argument against passive or backdrop conceptions of space-time. I do not wish to deny the bare possibility of a totally passive background to the events of the world. But it is difficult to believe that such a backdrop could play a serious explanatory role in physics and cosmology.

I will finish this discussion of the Causal argument by pointing out that it suggests an eirenic way of holding an ostensibly non-Naturalist theory of possibility which is actually compatible with Naturalism. Go back again to the upholder of the eccentric form of the Representative theory where physical objects are thought to have no effect on minds, and so are not causes of sense-data. Such a theorist, I argued, would have no good reason to postulate a physical world.

One thing that an upholder of this strange theory could do would be to identify physical objects with (collections of) sense-impressions. Such a course would be approved of by Berkeley, for instance. But suppose that such a theorist rejected the Berkeleian remedy, yet also became persuaded that he had no good reason to postulate a world of physical objects lying beyond the sense-impressions.

He could still argue that the conception of such a world was a useful conception. Let him agree that, because the world does not act on minds, he has no reason to think that such a world actually exists. Still, he may say, to refer, or better *ostensibly* to refer, our sense-data to such a world is a good way, methodologically speaking, to deal with these sense-data. We find it far easier to think and speak about the flow of our perceptions if we think and speak about them as, for the most part, perceptions of independently existing physical objects.

Might we not introduce possible worlds in the same spirit?

Physical scientists find such conceptions as the ideal gas useful in organizing their talk and calculations about actual gasses. They do not think that the ideal gas exists, either in this or in another world. Nevertheless, they distinguish between true and false statements about the ideal gas. It is true that it obeys Boyle's law. The ideal gas is only one example among many. Consider also point-masses, parallelograms of forces, frictionless planes, perfectly elastic bodies, economic man and so on. Why should not philosophers, including Naturalist philosophers, treat possible worlds in this fashion? They have proved their worth in discussions of problems about possibility and necessity, counterfactuals, personal identity and so on. Nevertheless, they lack *explanatory* value, just as the ideal gas lacks explanatory value. So why not treat possible worlds as we treat the ideal gas: as things which do not exist, or at least as things which we have no reason to postulate, but which it is nevertheless convenient (if ontologically misleading) to talk about?

It does seem like getting things on the cheap. But the widespread and practically essential device of *unrealistic idealization* in natural science suggests that the practice is not a disreputable one. Realism is better than Fictionalism – provided Realism is not carried too far. A realistic account of ideal gasses is not required. Why require a realistic theory of possible worlds? The Combinatorial theory to be developed in this work is a *Fictionalist* version of Combinatorialism.

2

Non-Naturalist
theories of possibility

The view now to be criticized is that, while ours is the only actual world, there do exist, in some sense of the word 'exist', merely possible worlds, set in one-to-one correspondence to, indeed constituting, the ways that the actual world might have been. It may or may not have been the view of Leibniz, but it is convenient to call it the Leibnizian view. It involves two levels of existence: the actual and the merely possible.

There exists a strong argument against this view, first stated, as far as I know, by D. C. Williams. It has since been endorsed by David Lewis, who heard the argument from Williams. I was told about it by Lewis.

Williams says:

There is no more thorough-paced philosopher than Leibniz, and the relations of essence and existence are the very crux of his system; yet he tells us almost nothing about Existence except that it is contingent and a predicate, and he half retracts these. He never intimates, for example, how he can tell that *he* is a member of the existent world and not a mere possible monad on the shelf of essence. (1962, p. 751–2)

It is illuminating, and convenient, to spell out the argument as a *proportional syllogism*:

(1) All but one of the infinity of worlds are merely possible (hypothesis)
(2) This is a world (containing Leibniz, the propounder of the argument, etc.)

∴ (very probably)

(3) This world is merely possible.

However, the conclusion (3) is absurd. It is obvious that this world is actual. So we have good reason to reject (1) as false.

The probability involved here is a *logical* probability, and as such it is relative to the premisses. As a result, it is subject to the well-known *total-evidence* condition. The premisses by themselves establish an overwhelming probability. But perhaps we have other knowledge or rational belief which enables us to reject (3)?

What then of our knowledge or rational belief that this world is actual which was used to negate (3)? We may not have any *evidence* for this proposition. But is it not part of bedrock common sense? Is it not one of those Moorean propositions of whose truth we are far more assured than any premiss in any philosophical argument that may be brought against it? Is it not properly part of our 'total evidence'?

It seems, however, that *once (1) is granted* this assurance must evaporate, and so cannot be incorporated into the total evidence. For given (1) then it follows that there are innumerable possible worlds where people take it to be bedrock common sense that they are actual. Yet there is only one of these worlds where their opinion is true. *In such a context,* assurance of actuality is worthless. At the same time, however, it remains open to common sense to use our assurance of actuality to *modus tollens* the argument, and so take (1) to be false. And that seems vastly preferable to accepting (1).

Ad hominem against Leibniz, if the sole actual world is the best of all possible worlds, as he maintained, then, granted (1), it is all the more likely that this world is a merely possible world.

Lewis, of course, is driven by the argument to his more thoroughgoing theory, the indexical theory of the actuality of worlds. The Williams argument has no force against his position. To Lewis's theory, therefore, we now turn.

II IS ACTUALITY INDEXICAL?

Lewis holds, as every Realist about possible worlds holds, that other possible worlds are never spatio-temporally or causally related to our world. Some other worlds *resemble* our world, but resemblance is an internal relation, determined solely by the nature of the objects related. It does not involve these objects being in any way connected. Lewis is not sure whether he should analyse resemblance in terms of universals. He is sure that, if he does admit universals, he will admit instantiated universals only (instantiated in *some* world). If universal U is instantiated in W_1 and W_2 (some-

15

thing is U in both worlds), then there is a certain identity across worlds. But there is still no path from world to world, and worlds do not affect each other.

Not only, however, does Lewis hold with everybody else that different possible worlds are spatio-temporally and causally cut off from each other, but he also converts the proposition. What is spatio-temporally and causally cut off from some other things is merely possible relative to these other things (and these other things merely possible relative to it). What is isolated from us is a mere possibility relative to us, and we a mere possibility relative to the isolated realm.

This doctrine is perhaps rather surprising, but Lewis does not hold it lightly. As we shall see in Section VII of this chapter, if he did not hold it, he would at least find it more difficult to meet a certain criticism which tries to demonstrate a contradiction in his view of possible worlds. In this present section, however, I will simply accept what he says, but argue that the resulting position is implausible.

For Lewis, the spatio-temporal and causal isolation (hencefor-ward 'isolation') of worlds *constitutes* their being merely possible relative to each other. He cannot say that the notions of isolation and relative possibility are merely extensionally equivalent! They are the same thing. But, I object, there is no reason to think that what is isolated from us is merely possible relative to us. On the contrary, if it exists, then it is real; it is actual.

Before ever having heard of Lewis's ideas about possibility I, like many other philosophers, had considered the question whether there might be another spatio-temporal system completely cut off from ours. Kant had denied the possibility, but Kant's denial is, perhaps, bound up with idiosyncratic, and anti-Realist, features of his system. C. D. Broad, however, in the course of an argument to show that the principle of the Identity of Indiscernibles is not a necessary truth, argued that spatio-temporal systems entirely cut off from each other are a logical possibility (Broad 1933, pp. 176–7). I read Broad on the point, and thought he was right. I still do so. But I did not think of such 'island universes' (to borrow Edwin Hubble's phrase for the galaxies) as anything but *actual* relative to our spatio-temporal system. Neither did Broad.

It is intuitively natural, then, to describe what Lewis has done as the expanding of the dimensions of the actual. The actual is expanded so far that every possibility for a space-time is actual in some island universe. There are no *mere* possibilities. Nor would I deny the logical possibility that the actual has these swollen dimensions. But I see no reason to think that this is the way that the actual really is. One of the possibilities for the actual is that every possible spatio-temporal system exists. But it is only one possibility.[1]

It is true that Lewis's 'multiverse', as we might call it, is a philosophically useful conception. It is useful because each possibility for *our* spatio-temporal system is modelled by an island universe. But as already suggested at the end of the preceding chapter, we need not credit such island universes with being. They are useful *fictions*.

III COUNTERPARTS

Lewis maintains that individuals – first-order particulars – do not occur in more than one world. He has been criticized for this, notably by Kripke (1980). Lewis's doctrine seems not to accord with ordinary language. We may say of somebody who failed in his enterprise that it is possible that *he* should have brought it off. But Lewis will only allow that, in some other world, his *counterpart*, somebody who resembles him, brings it off. We might stigmatize this as a waxwork account of identity across worlds. I may say of somebody recently become famous: 'He is now in Madame Tussaud's'. But, of course, he is not, or he need not be. Only his simulacrum is there.

Lewis may, and does, argue that his counterpart theory analyses, or gives the truth-conditions for, statements about mere possibilities for individuals in this world, and so, trivially, is *about* these individuals. Hubert Humphrey did not, but might have, become president of the United States. That statement is true, says Lewis. What makes it true is the states of affairs in other worlds where

---

1 If this possibility is actual, however, then a doctrine I uphold, as contingently true, viz. Naturalism, is false. For I define Naturalism as the doctrine that all that exists is a *single* (i.e. unified) space-time. I take the Causal argument of Section II of the preceding chapter to be an argument for Naturalism so defined. Notice that the so-called many-worlds interpretation of quantum physics suggested by some contemporary physicists does not contradict Naturalism. For the most that is envisaged is a continued branching from the one world. This I would count (in agreement with Lewis as it happens) as a theory of a single space-time, but one of an unorthodox shape.

Humphrey counterparts win the presidency of counterparts of the United States.

But it must surely be admitted that this is a thoroughly Pickwickian or deflationary account of what it is for it to be true that Humphrey might have won. It is similar to Berkeley's account of the physical world. Berkeley may protest that he does not deny the existence, not even the unobserved existence, of gloves and cherries. But his account of what it is for them to exist, and, even more, what it is for them to exist unobserved, is so deflationary that it is a form of such a denial. Similarly for Lewis. The 'identity across worlds' which he allows is not *really* identity across worlds.

We have already seen that (give or take uncertainty about the existence of universals) Lewis is prepared to allow that individuals in different worlds may instantiate the very same universal. So why does he not allow that individuals in different worlds may be strictly identical, though perhaps instantiating different universals? Lewis himself says that this view is 'agreeably simple' (1986a, p. 199).

Lewis rejects (genuine) transworld identity of individuals because of what he calls *the problem of accidental intrinsics* (1986a, 4.2). There is no problem, he thinks, in exactly the same individuals having different relational properties in different worlds. Hubert Humphrey could own just five dogs in one world, just six dogs in another. For these different properties involve no difference in Humphrey himself. Again, there is no problem in those of Humphrey's non-relational (i.e. intrinsic) properties that do not change from world to world: his essential properties, if he has any. But how can Humphrey have incompatible intrinsic properties at different worlds? He cannot, Lewis argues, any more than he can have incompatible intrinsic properties in this world. Humphrey would have to be different from himself!

It may be replied that Humphrey can, and does, have incompatible intrinsic properties even in this world. Substances admit contraries, Aristotle said. They do this by having different properties at different times. For instance, Humphrey is not always at the same temperature.

But in Lewis's opinion (with which I agree) this temporal situation raises just as serious a problem of incompatible intrinsic properties as does the case of identity across worlds. In Lewis's view we must solve the problem by admitting temporal parts of Humphrey.

(Again, I agree.) It is different temporal parts of Humphrey which differ in temperature. Applied to the case of identity across worlds this would destroy the strict identity desired. For it is Humphrey, *this man here,* or, indeed, this man here at this moment, who could have been other than he was.

There are various alleged ways out to be considered. Lewis considers, and rejects, for instance, the attempt to construe intrinsic properties as relations between individuals and worlds. I will simply say that I find his very thorough discussion entirely convincing.

Lewis's identity across worlds, then, is an *Ersatz* identity, and I agree with him that he cannot do better. Can other theories do better? In particular, what of non–Realist theories? The central insight, as I take it to be, of non–Realist theories is that what is merely possible does not exist (or subsist, or have any sort of being). Consider the false proposition that Humphrey has six fingers on his left hand, the example being chosen because it involves 'accidental intrinsics'. Humphrey exists all right (past existence is existence), and the proposition shows every sign of being literally about *him.* But the state of affairs of Humphrey's having six fingers on his left hand does not exist. As a result, there is no spectre of a six-fingers-on-the-left-hand Humphrey to compete with the actual Humphrey.

Nevertheless, we can refer to this non–existent state of affairs. Or better, to try to avoid a taint of 'Meinongianism', we can make *ostensible* reference to this state of affairs; we can 'make as if' there is such a state of affairs. What is more we can (apparently) classify this state of affairs as a *possible* one. The principles involved in this classification are, according to me, combinatorial, combinatorial on elements in the actual world. I will be trying to spell out these principles in the body of this essay. But regardless of our *particular* non–Realist theory of possibility, it seems that non–Realist theories can construe the proposition about Humphrey as being literally about him. Whatever strikes there may be against such theories, this is a score for them. It is therefore a point of superiority to Lewis's theory.

IV   THE PLENITUDE OF WORLDS

Realists about possible worlds characteristically assume that there are vast numbers of these worlds. But Peter van Inwagen has pointed out, and the point has been accepted by Lewis (1986a, 1.8), that in default of extra principles there is no justification for this assumption in the theory. Perhaps, as Lewis says, there are only seventeen possible worlds. What principles entitle him to assume that this result is false?

Lewis suggests that we should appeal to a *Principle of Recombination* (p. 87). This principle draws its inspiration from Hume's principle that there are no necessary connections between distinct existences. Any two distinct existences may be found together, or found one without the other, in a single world. Think of our world as like a patchwork quilt, with the individual patches as the distinct existences. Any recombination of the patches will be a possible world. 'Recombination' of patches here can be taken to include *subtraction* of patches from the quilt and the *indefinite reduplication* of any patch.

As explained so far, the principle is still purely formal because it does not tell us what the distinct existences, the individual patches, are. But Lewis suggests that the paradigms of distinct existence are those things which occupy distinct spatio-temporal positions. It may be that things can occupy the very same position, and yet be distinct existences. But that is a question for further and difficult investigation. The things which occupy distinct spatio-temporal positions, on the other hand, are secure examples of distinct existences. They are the secure examples of distinct patches of the quilt.

At this point it should be noticed that the phrase 'indefinite reduplication' is a little too liberal from Lewis's point of view. Lewis does require that a world be a spatio-temporal unity. He does not put strong conditions on what constitutes such a unity. For instance, if a world branched at a certain point of time, but thereafter the branches lacked any spatial or other external relation, this would be acceptable to Lewis as a single world. But indefinite reduplication must not permit the putative possible world to lack all spatio-temporal unity.

(My own view, as already indicated in Section II of this chapter, is that Lewis's view is still too strong. A possible world need not have any sort of unity. It might consist of two or more island universes. This disagreement will become important again in Section VII.)

Now I do not wish to contest Lewis's Principle of Recombination, except in such matters of comparative detail. It seems to me to be a correct principle. But what I do want to emphasize is the point which Lewis is perfectly candid about: that his general realistic theory of possible worlds, and his Principle of Recombination, are independent of each other. Suppose, then, that we can develop a theory of possibility which *starts* from, and derives the developed theory from, the idea of recombination. That will be a considerable intellectual economy, and a considerable intellectual recommendation. The positive theory to be developed in Part II of this essay is just such a theory.

Before concluding this section, it should be noticed that Lewis does not simply rely on the Principle of Recombination to yield the infinities of possible worlds which it seems natural to postulate (if we postulate possible worlds at all). He also argues for the possibility of an indefinite number of *alien* properties and relations (pp. 91–2). Recombination includes reduplication, and so alien *individuals* are automatically given by recombination. Alien properties and relations are a further matter, however. A property which is alien (relative to this world) may be defined as one which is wholly other than, wholly different from, any property to be found in this world, or one which contains such a wholly other element. The same goes for alien relations.

If an indefinite multitude of alien properties and relations is allowed, then this will indefinitely enlarge the materials available for forming new worlds.

Postulating alien properties and relations in other possible worlds is plausible. And once the postulation is made, they constitute a strong argument for a Realistic theory of possibilities. For what else could serve as a truth-maker or ontological ground for the assertion that there are such possibilities? It is just for this reason that, when I come to develop my own view, I shall deny that there are such alien possibilities. I grant the plausibility of postulating them. But their existence is certainly not part of that Moorean common sense which philosophers deny at their peril. A theory which is plausible on other grounds can afford the somewhat counter-intuitive denial of alien properties and relations. In any case, I believe that the plausibility of the intuition in favour of these alien possibilities can be explained away. The matter may be left for the present.

A question which can be raised about Lewis's theory is whether or not he should admit *indiscernible* worlds. Are there worlds which are perfect twins, perfect duplicates, of each other?

Lewis himself, when he considers this question, says, 'I have no idea whether there are indiscernible worlds' (1986a, p. 84). (He does add, correctly I think, that there certainly are indiscernible parts of worlds. The latter conclusion falls straight out of the Principle of Recombination.) His idea is that a Realist about possible worlds should not pretend to settle such a question from his armchair in just one of them.

It seems, however, that there is a certain pressure on Lewis to admit that there *are* indiscernible worlds. His possible worlds are, relative to each other, 'distinct existences' in the Humean sense. It is a mark of a distinct existence, at least according to Hume, that it permits the existence of any further distinct existence, including discernible duplicates. I believe, indeed, that this is a true principle of the theory of possibility. But in a Realistic treatment of possibility, what is permitted exists. So should there not be indiscernible worlds?

Lewis would object that the Principle of Recombination permits him to recombine and reduplicate things *within a world*. It takes things which are not side by side in one world and places them side by side in another. For instance, given a world, it would permit a world consisting of two duplicates of the original world united in a single space-time. (As Lewis suggests elsewhere, they – the duplicates – might have only a single space-time point in common.) But the principle is silent on whether worlds themselves can have duplicates.

But is this not an arbitrary restriction of recombination? It would certainly seem to be an arbitrary restriction of Hume's principle. And if one works with a restricted principle, as Lewis does, is it not natural to extend that principle to allow the duplication of worlds? After all, he insists that worlds are *concrete* entities. Why not two exactly alike?

So let us suppose that Lewis admits indiscernible worlds. This creates two problems for him. One is minor, but the other more serious.

The minor problem is this. Each of his worlds is supposed to be a possibility for a world: a way that a world could be. Such possibilities, however, obey the principle of the Identity of Indiscernibles. There cannot be two or more such possibilities which are identical in content. (There is the possibility of duplication, but not the duplication of possibilities.) But are not indiscernible worlds reduplications of the same possibility?

Lewis can deal with this difficulty reasonably well. He can modify his theory minimally and identify a possibility for a world with an equivalence class of indiscernible worlds. Or, still more satisfactorily, if he is prepared to admit structural universals[2] he can identify a possibility for a world with that complex structural universal which makes each member of a set of indiscernible worlds indiscernible from each other.

The other difficulty is more troublesome. If there are indiscernible worlds, then presumably each world is a member of such a (plural) set. Presumably also, on pain of the greatest arbitrariness, each such set will have the same number. This number will be indefinitely large: The sets will be denumerable sets at least. But why should we stop at the lowest infinity? Humean considerations drive us on. But where then do we stop? There is no highest infinity. Any choice will seem arbitrarily restrictive.

In answer to another difficulty, to be discussed in Section VII of this chapter, Lewis suggests that in the procession of the infinite cardinals some 'natural break' may be identified. If there is such a number, then it might be thought (speculatively) to be the number of the classes of indiscernible worlds. This, however, is as far as Lewis goes. He has no concrete suggestion as to what that number might be. It is to be noted, furthermore, that there he is concerned with the question, What is the biggest world which can be fitted into a single space-time? By contrast, once he has admitted that there are indiscernible worlds, it is hard to see what restriction will stop them multiplying indefinitely. It is therefore hard to see what would constitute a natural stopping point.

I think Lewis ought to deal with this dilemma by denying that there can, after all, be indiscernible worlds. But as we have seen, he is then in some bind. For a principle which he himself recognizes the force of, the Principle of Recombination, seems to push him towards admitting indiscernible worlds.

---

2 A type of universal that Lewis finds particularly dubious. See his 1986b.

There is a consequence of Lewis's theory which deserves notice. It is not logically possible for there to be nothing at all. For on Lewis's theory this would have become a *world* in which there was nothing at all. But that does not differ from the absence of a world (1986a, pp. 73–4).

What should we say of this consequence? There are a great many philosophers who hold that there could have been nothing at all. For them, this consequence may be an objection to Lewis's theory. But how solid is their opinion?

Notice that their view is certainly not a basic commonsense belief of the sort which is, in general, much more certain than any train of philosophical reasoning which seems to cast doubt on it. I remember that when I was first introduced in philosophy to the idea that there might have been nothing at all, I found it a novel conception, and surprising. I came to accept it, but as the result of a short train of philosophical reasoning. The proposition that there might have been nothing at all cannot claim any 'Moorean privilege'.

The reasoning that influenced me, and I think many others, was this. The first premiss is that the world is exclusively a world of contingent beings. But any contingent being might not have existed. So could it not have been the case that the totality of contingent beings failed to exist? There might have been nothing at all.

All philosophers are perfectly aware that this may be (doxastic 'may be') an invalid line of reasoning. An army can exist without any particular soldier of that army. Yet it cannot exist without any soldiers at all. So, perhaps, although there can be a world without any particular being, there cannot be a world without anything at all. But, I think, many of these philosophers have also thought that, in default of some special reason for thinking that the move from 'each thing might not have existed' to 'nothing might have existed' is invalid, it is reasonable to assume it *is* valid.

Fair enough. But if from a *well-worked-out theory of possibility* the conclusion drops out that it is not possible that there should be nothing at all, a new complexion has been put on matters. Now a reason has been given. The *prima facie* case for saying that there might have been nothing at all does not now have the same weight.

I confess that I have an interest in putting forward these apologetics on Lewis's behalf. For the theory of possibility which I favour, the theory to be put forward in Part II, also has the consequence that it is not possible that there could have been nothing at all. Indeed, this consequence shows a tendency to fall out of *worked-out* theories of possibility. I believe that the idea that there could have been nothing at all is really a *superficial* idea. It is attractive at a relatively shallow level of reflection. But when we think more deeply about the nature of possibility, then, it seems, it has to be given up.

VII THE FORREST–ARMSTRONG ARGUMENT

Peter Forrest and I (Forrest and Armstrong 1984) have developed an argument whose objective is to show that Lewis's system of possible worlds, together with a certain assumption that he makes, is likely to involve a contradiction.

Consider two of Lewis's worlds. It seems clear that there exists a third world which stands to the first two worlds in the following way. This third world is exhaustively divisible into two non-overlapping parts, P_1 and P_2. P_1 is internally indiscernible from, is an internal duplicate of, is, in a phrase suggested by Fred Dretske, an internal mirror image of the first world (but without left–right reversal!). P_2 similarly duplicates the second world. This construction is an application of a plausible principle of recombination.

This style of reasoning is then used to show that there is no *set* and equally no *aggregate* of the possible worlds.

The argument proceeds by *reductio ad absurdum*. Suppose that there *is* such a set and call it C. Now consider a very big world, W_B, having the following nature. It may be divided into proper parts, *P*, which do not overlap with each other. For each world, W, in C, there exists in W_B a *P* which is an internal duplicate of that W. As will be shown immediately, W_B is not a member of C. This reduces the hypothesis that C exists to absurdity.

Here is the proof. Consider a world W_1, and let it contain *n* electrons. Like any other world, there will be modal truths which hold of W_1. In particular, there will be some property, *F-ness,* relational or non-relational, which each electron in W_1 may have, or may not have, and may have it or not have it *independently of whether the other electrons in W_1 have it or do not have it*. This means that, for *each* subset of the *n* electrons, it is possible that the members of the subset, and they alone, have F-ness.

This in turn means that C (a set of worlds, not itself a world) must contain distinct possible worlds containing electrons, with a world corresponding to each of the subsets of the set of n electrons in W_1. Each world could be exactly like W_1, except that, in each of them, F-ness is added to the members of just one of the subsets of electrons, a different subset for each world. As Lewis points out (1986a, p. 102), this is a further use of the Principle of Recombination. There are 2^n of these worlds. Hence the number of the electrons in the totality of worlds that are members of C is at least 2^n.

Return now to consider the big world W_B. It contains, as non-overlapping parts, a duplicate (internal mirror image) of *each* world in C. So W_B contains 2^n electrons. But 2^n is a greater number than n, even for infinite cardinals. As a result W_B has more electrons than W_1, the member of C with just n electrons. By the same argument, W_B has more electrons than any other world in C. So W_B is not a member of C. But C was supposed to be the set of *all* possible worlds.

An exactly parallel argument shows that there is no such thing as the *aggregate* of all possible worlds. There is no big thing of which they are all parts.

The first thing to be considered about this argument is whether Lewis can simply accept its conclusion, and deny that there is a set and aggregate of the worlds. In fact, he is totally unwilling to do this, and offers a number of reasons for not doing it (1986a, p. 104). What I take to be his central point is this. His modal realism commits him to the existence of objectively existing, indexically actual, worlds, each a distinct existence from the others, and on the same ontological level. How could they fail to form a set? And equally, how could they fail to form an aggregate?

If, then, Lewis cannot accept the conclusion of the argument, how should he respond to it? Before considering his actual response, I will suppose that he allows as a logical possibility something which he explicitly rejects as a possibility. I have already argued in Section II that the one world could contain different 'island universes' which are completely cut off from each other, being neither causally nor spatio-temporally related. I think that this is a way that a world could be. It is possible that our world is like this, although we have no actual reason to think it is. Lewis rejects this view, of course. For him, island universes are different

26

possible worlds relative to each other. But it is instructive to consider the Forrest–Armstrong argument when applied to a Lewis-type theory which, in contrast to Lewis, allows island universes within a single world.

The immediate effect of allowing such islanded worlds is to strengthen the Forrest–Armstrong argument. This argument works by taking the alleged set or aggregate of possible worlds and then setting up a world, W_B, with non-overlapping parts which duplicate each member of the set (or world in the aggregate). It is then argued that W_B is not in the set (aggregate). If these non-overlapping parts can each be island universes, then it is particularly plausible to argue that W_B is a possible world.

What could Lewis do? Since he allows (correctly, from the standpoint of his theory) that the worlds do form a set and an aggregate, what he would have to do is to argue that at some point we reach a collection of worlds which cannot be mapped into a single world in this way. Some putative worlds are too big to be possible. But when is this point reached? When can the combinatorial explosion be stopped? The problem is the same as the problem Lewis has if he allows indiscernible worlds (see Section V of this chapter). Whatever infinity of indiscernible worlds is allowed, why not a higher infinity? But in the case of the indiscernible worlds Lewis at least has the option of denying that there are any indiscernible worlds at all. No such way out is available for the present problem. Lewis would have to hope for some 'natural break' in the procession of the infinite cardinals, a break yielding a cardinal which could be tentatively and speculatively identified with the greatest number of the possible worlds.

Lewis escapes from this unappetizing situation by holding that a single world, if it is to be a single world, must be a spatio-temporal unity. He does not intend 'spatio-temporal unity' to be taken too restrictively. For instance, minds which are in time but not in space (a Dualist conception which Lewis holds to be a logical possibility for the mind, although not an actuality) would be admitted. A world must be united by a structure which is something like the spatio-temporal structure of our world.

Given this view, it becomes more plausible to argue that there is an upper limit to the number of entities (excluding sets) that a world contains, a conclusion that blocks the Forrest–Armstrong argument. For there may well be a limit to what can be packed into a structure which resembles a spatio-temporal structure. As Lewis puts it:

> Among the mathematical structures that might be offered as isomorphs of possible spacetimes, some would be admitted, and others would be rejected as oversized. (1986a, p. 103)

For instance, Lewis says, a restriction to four, or to seventeen, dimensions looks quite arbitrary. But, it may be, a restriction to space-time–like structures with only a finite number of dimensions is less arbitrary. Lewis is not dogmatic about the last point. Perhaps we will want to admit an infinite number of dimensions as a possibility. But if so, to give the view any plausibility, there will have to be some natural break higher up.

So the theory requires that there is some natural break. Lewis does not claim to know where that break is, and if subsequent mathematical investigation showed that no such break exists, then that, he concedes, would be serious trouble for the theory. If a *number* of such breaks exist, then that would not worry Lewis. It would simply mean that it is not possible to discover which in particular is the break which marks the biggest sort of possible world.

His position, however, is not so difficult as it would be if he admits indiscernible worlds and then faces the problem of how many tokens exist of each world-type. With the latter problem, he needs to find a natural break just in the series of the infinite cardinals. The same would apply if he admitted 'island universes' into a single world. But now he requires only a plausible and natural answer to the question what is the biggest size possible for a world that is (broadly) spatio-temporal. Such an answer may be more attainable.

Nevertheless, Lewis has still given a considerable hostage to intellectual fortune. And he has to maintain in addition, what I have maintained to be implausible, that a single world cannot contain island universes. He has further to maintain, what seems not to be a necessary truth, that a possible world must have a structure which bears an analogy to the structure of space-time.

We have now seen that the Forrest–Armstrong argument creates problems for Lewis. But before leaving the discussion, it ought to be considered what conclusions should be drawn from the argument for the theory of possibility generally.

I think the argument does show that there is no set (or aggregate) of possible worlds. Given a world with n wholly distinct elements (the importance of the 'wholly' will energe at a later point in this essay), we can combine the elements to form 2^n possible worlds. Then we can construct a single world having non–overlapping parts, with a part to duplicate each of the 2^n worlds. This world has 2^n wholly distinct elements at least, so it is bigger than any world in the original set of 2^n worlds. And since this procedure is available for *any* set of possible worlds, there is no all–embracing set (or aggregate) of such worlds.

The obvious parallel is with set theory. We know that there is no set of all sets. Nevertheless, there is an *iterative* procedure which shows us that, given a set, we can go on to form a higher-order set with a higher cardinality than the original set. Iterative set theory, which is contradiction-free as far as we know, provides a respectable way of talking about sets (see Boolos 1971).

What we must accept, therefore, is an iterative conception of possible worlds. Given any world, in particular the actual world, Combinatorial principles deliver further worlds. But any attempt to form the set of all such worlds is defeated by a procedure which uses the given set to form worlds outside the set.

Lewis, of course, cannot accept an iterative theory of possible worlds. For him, all worlds must be, as it were, equal and independent. Worlds are not reached *through* worlds. Iteration demands a base from which to start the iterative process. For an Actualist, the actual world can provide such a base. Lewis has no base. Recombination practiced on our world may, for Lewis, tell us about the nature of some of the other worlds. But it cannot be constitutive of other worlds that they are thus built up from a base in our world. So he must accept that there is a set of all possible worlds.

One question remains: If we accept an iterative view of possible worlds, and so deny that there is a set or aggregate of such worlds, can we continue, in good conscience, to speak about *all* possible worlds? We want to do the latter, at least if we want to define necessary truth as truth in all possible worlds.

What we must deny is that the universal quantifier here ranges over a *set* of things. It is not at all obvious, however, that the range of a quantifier cannot be wider than this. If, for instance, a distinction can be drawn between sets and classes, with classes the wider notion, then the quantifier might range over all classes.

I believe that a reasonably strong case against Lewis's theory has been made out. First, like other non-Naturalist theories, it involves postulating entities which are causally and nomically impotent in the (actual) space-time world. I argued that this was a major disadvantage. It was suggested, however, that this disadvantage might largely be cancelled if the Lewis worlds were treated as fictions, things useful to talk about in the same way that it is useful to talk about ideal gasses and other fictional scientific entities.

Second, I criticized Lewis's view that for a world to be merely possible relative to another world, it is sufficient that it be totally cut off from the second world, lacking any spatio-temporal or causal relations to that world. *One* world could contain a multitude of 'island universes'. 'Actual' is not an indexical term relative to the spatio-temporal system in which, and about which, the term is used.

Third, given the real existence of the Lewisian possible worlds, it appears that statements of mere possibility about this-worldly individuals must be interpreted as really being about their counterparts in other worlds. This is an implausible account of such statements.

Fourth, Lewis's theory gives us no guide as to what worlds are possible. Extra principles, in particular a Hume-inspired Principle of Recombination, must be appealed to if we are to have any view about the nature and number of the worlds. The theory is to that extent unproductive and uneconomical.

Fifth, Lewis has a problem about whether to admit indiscernible worlds. The Principle of Recombination speaks in favour of admitting them. But if they are admitted, it is hard to put any non-arbitrary figure on the number to be admitted.

Sixth, given plausible Combinatorial principles, Lewis cannot give sense to, yet needs to give sense to, the notion of the set and/or aggregate of all possible worlds. He cannot accept an *iterative* theory of possible worlds because for him there can be no hierarchy of worlds.

IX NON-NATURALIST ACTUALISM

We come now to what Lewis calls *Ersatz* accounts of possibilities and possible worlds. Such accounts accept only one actual world, nor do they, even, like the Leibnizian view, admit merely possible worlds. For these *Actualists* certain actual entities *represent* or may be used to represent possibilities, including whole worlds. If the possibilities are actual, or if the possible world in question is the actual world, then something corresponds to these representations. But otherwise not.

The question then shifts to the nature of these representing entities. A Naturalist will wish to take them as purely natural entities, things which lie within the spatio-temporal system. If this could be done satisfactorily, it would be a particularly economical solution. But the Actualist may think that the representing entities required are not to be found in the world of nature. If so, then he is a non-Naturalist Actualist. Theories of this sort are our present business.

I am much more in sympathy with non-Naturalist Actualism than I am with a Lewisian or Leibnizian Modal Realism. Actualist views respect what I take to be the crucial insight: that the merely possible does not exist. As a result, I have less to criticize, and less to say, then I have about Lewis's views. But the Naturalist must be sharply conscious that these forms of Actualism are metaphysically uneconomical theories.

A way to develop such a form of Actualism is to postulate the existence of *objective propositions*. These are not sentences but, rather, the *meanings* of sentences, where any difference in truth-condition constitutes a difference in meaning, and where the meanings exist independently of any expression in sentences. These represent possibilities. As indicated by Adams (1974), a *world-story* can then be defined as a maximally consistent set of propositions. A world-story represents a possible world.

It seems important that propositions and world-stories not be taken to be possibilities and possible worlds, or even *substitutes* for possibilities and possible worlds. Lewis takes them to be substitutes, and so thinks of a theory like Adams's as an *Ersatz* theory. (He, Lewis, has the real thing.) But, as I see it, an Actualist should say that (mere) possibilities do not exist. Propositions and world-stories *represent* possibilities, but are themselves actualities.

We may begin by considering what advantages the theory has over Lewis's theory. In the first place, I would put the fact that it is an Actualist, or one-world theory.

Second, Lewis's worlds lie under strong suspicion of themselves being actual, even if far away. No such charge can be laid against non-Naturalist Actualism.

31

Third, the view appears to have no trouble with the identity of actual individuals across possible worlds. The propositions postulated by the theory may be mysterious entities. But if they exist, then surely some of them involve essential reference to actual particulars. Propositions of this sort are available for inclusion in maximal consistent sets.

Fourth, this theory has an advantage over Lewis's theory on the question of indiscernible worlds. A maximally consistent set of propositions yields only the one world for the one set of propositions. This is just the result wanted.

Fifth, non-Naturalist Actualism can give some account of the possibility of an empty world. In some theories of this sort objective propositions are necessary beings. But at least there is a contradictory pair of propositions: 'Something contingent exists', and 'It is not the case that something contingent exists'. Taking the latter, and taking no further proposition which is inconsistent with it, it seems that we can make it part of a maximally consistent set of propositions. This set represents a world which is empty at least of contingent beings.

Sixth, there seems to be no reason why the non-Naturalist Actualist should not accept an iterative account of how certain maximally consistent sets of propositions are formed. The Forrest–Armstrong objection to Lewis's view is therefore no objection here.

But now to mention some difficulties.

First, if these propositions are 'abstract', that is to say outside the natural order, then they will be causally and nomically impotent with respect to the natural world. This was the objection urged in Chapter 1, Section II, against all non-Naturalist theories. Nothing in the spatio-temporal world, including our mental processes, is a manifestation of these entities. Why then should we postulate them?

In the case of Lewis's worlds, we saw that one might entertain the idea of a fictionalist version of his theory. The worlds do not exist, but it may be useful to talk about them. A fictionalist treatment of 'abstract' propositions seems to have little to recommend it. Why not go straight to a fictionalist treatment of the things that the maximally consistent sets represent, namely the worlds?

Second, there is the question of the plenitude of worlds. We saw that Lewis's theory does not by itself yield any particular view of the number and nature of the worlds (Section IV). He has to introduce an independent principle, the Principle of Recombination, to yield the multitude of possibilities and possible worlds which it seems natural to allow.

Non-Naturalist Actualism is in the same position. Apart from our more or less pre-theoretical modal intuitions, the theory gives us no guidance as to the number and the nature of the maximally consistent sets of propositions.

But third, as pointed out by Lewis (1986a, pp. 150–7), non-Naturalist Actualism must not only be supplemented by giving further principles which govern modality, but it must also take the fact of modality as primitive. For a set of propositions to represent a world, it is a necessary condition that the sets be *consistent*. But this is a modal notion: Consistency means that it is *possible* for all members of the set to be true together. Further, the set must be *maximally* consistent. This means that it is *not possible* to add further propositions to the set without destroying consistency. So the theory provides no *analysis* of modality.

The Leibnizian and Lewisian theories, of course, do not take modality as primitive.[3] They set up worlds, and can then analyse a notion such as consistency. Propositions p and q are consistent if and only if there are worlds where both propositions are true (or, if the propositions involve actual individuals, and identity of individuals across worlds is denied, worlds where corresponding propositions hold of close counterparts of these individuals).

Lewis argues (1986a, p. 156) that this lack of analysis of modality is no fatal objection to non-Naturalist Actualism. It is not unreasonable that a modal metaphysician should treat the basic notion of modality as primitive, and so seek to do no more than give a systematic theory of it. It is ontological diseconomy, of course, but perhaps, contrary to Lewis's hopes, it is a diseconomy which cannot be avoided.

I agree with Lewis up to a point. Perhaps modality is an unanalysable primitive. But if it is, why introduce a great deal of

---

3 The anonymous referee for Cambridge University Press pointed out that if Lewis were to allow 'island universes' as different parts of the one world, then he would apparently be compelled to reintroduce primitive modality. For how else could he sort out island universes that are co-actual, are world-mates, from those that do not bear this relation? So it seems that even more hangs on the island-universe question than I had previously thought.

causally impotent, and therefore metaphysically suspect, apparatus which does no more than systematize the facts about modality? Why not instead start from a Naturalist basis, and enrich the space-time world with modal features, making some this-worldly states of affairs contingent, others necessary? Such modal features are surely more attractive candidates for the truth-makers of modal truths than the propositions of the non-Naturalist actualists. The Combinatorial theory now to be argued for purports to give an *analysis* of modality in combinatorial terms. But if the analysis is circular, as I hope it is not, it might still be developed with modal primitives in a Naturalist context.

The case against non-Naturalist Actualism, then, rests on three points. First, there is the causal/nomic impotence of the entities postulated. Second, such a theory gives no guidance as to the actual content of the principles of modality. Third, despite its postulation of elaborate metaphysical machinery, the theory has to accept modality as a primitive, unanalysed, notion.

PART II

A Combinatorial and Naturalist account of possibility

3

Possibility in a simple world

The Naturalist theory of possibility now to be advanced will be called a Combinatorial theory. It traces the very idea of possibility to the idea of the combinations – *all* the combinations – of given, actual elements. Combination is to be understood widely. It includes the notions of expansion (perhaps 'repetition' is a less misleading term) and also contraction.

It is to be emphasized that the central idea is not original, although naturally I hope I will be making some contribution to the details. The central idea is in the *Tractatus,* and it is one of the central ideas of the *Tractatus.* Perhaps its charter is 3.4:

A proposition determines a place in logical space. The existence of this logical place is guaranteed by *the mere existence of the constituents.* [My italics.]

I myself encountered the Combinatorial idea, and was converted, in Brian Skyrms's article 'Tractarian Nominalism' (1981), which is reprinted at the end of this book as an appendix. But a Combinatorial conception of possibility was put forward earlier by Max Cresswell (1972) and before that at least toyed with, quite a vigorous toying, by Quine (1969, pp. 147–52). The Combinatorial theory of Cresswell and Quine does not involve the fictionalist element that mine will have.

I shall develop the theory in a particular way, a way determined by my own metaphysical views, in particular by my acceptance of (*in re*) universals (see Armstrong 1978a, b). It seems a peculiarly apt way to develop a Combinatorial theory. But I expect that a version of this theory of possibility could be developed by those who articulate their Naturalism in a different way than I do (in particular, those who are Nominalists) or, perhaps, who are not Naturalists at all.

The theory will be developed in stages, and not all that is said at the beginning will represent the final view to be presented. I will start with a view of the world which is, with the exception of its explicit recourse to universals, close to the *Tractatus* account. A Combinatorial theory of possibility for such a world will be developed. A conception of possible worlds will also be developed: Such worlds will be called the Wittgenstein worlds. After that, some ladders will have to be kicked away. The scheme must be added to, and in a degree modified, to yield a deeper view.

II SKETCH OF AN ONTOLOGY

The world I begin with contains a number of individuals (first-order particulars), *a, b, c* . . . . The number is not specified. It might be a finite number, it might be infinite (one of the infinite cardinals). I think that it is an empirical question, to be decided on *a posteriori,* scientific, grounds, if it can be decided at all, how many individuals the world contains.

We make the preliminary assumption, however, to be abstracted from subsequently, that these individuals are *simple.* The force of the word 'simple' must not be overestimated here. It does not mean that these individuals may not have indefinitely many properties, or stand in indefinitely many relations to indefinitely many other individuals. The simplicity of the individuals is constituted by the fact that they have no individuals as proper parts.

Candidates for such individuals would be point-instants, but point-instants which are conceived of not as 'bare' point-instants but as things having properties and standing in relations to other point-instants. If we so conceive of the individuals, then ordinary particulars will be complexes of such individuals, complexes having both spatial and *temporal* parts. But I stress that such point-instants are mere candidates for the simple individuals. Like Wittgenstein, my argument abstracts from the concrete nature of the individuals postulated.

The world also contains, in finite or infinite number, simple properties, F, G, ... The simplicity of simple properties is constituted by their lacking proper constituents, where a constituent of a property is itself a property, or, in the case of structural properties, a property or relation. The term 'constituent' replaces the term 'part' which I would once have used. This is because these constituents have a non-mereological relation to the properties and relations of which they are constituents. The word 'part' is best kept for the part-whole relation studied in mereology. More of this anon.

For the present, we are not endowing these properties with further properties or giving them relations to other properties. For the present, that is, we are not contemplating *higher-order* properties and relations.

These simple properties are conceived of as *universals*. By this is meant no more than that any property can be possessed by more than one, indeed by indefinitely many, individuals. If a is F, and if the distinct individual b is also F, then a and b are identical in this respect.

If F and G are properties, then there is no property of *being F or G*. Similarly there are no properties of *not being F* and *not being G*. There are no disjunctive or negative properties. The corresponding *predicates* exist, of course, and are likely to be applicable to various individuals. But properties are not to be conceived of as the meanings of predicates, and no simple relationship between predicates and properties can be assumed. Properties are universals, identical in different individuals.[1] But what properties there are is in no case to be determined *a priori*. It is to be determined empirically, *a posteriori,* on the basis of total science.

Finally, the world contains a finite or infinite number of relations, R, S, ... Like properties, they are universals. They are simple because they lack proper constituents, whether these constituents be relations or properties. They may be dyadic, tetradic, ... Indeed, I can think of no convincing *a priori* reason why the number of places in a simple relation should not be infinite, although I cannot imagine what an example would be like.

---

1 The argument to universals is perhaps best presented as an inference to the best explanation from the facts of resemblance, talk of sameness of sort and kind, the application of one predicate to an indefinite and unforeseen multitude of individuals, etc. See Swoyer (1983). Of course, it will have to be shown that it is the *best* explanation of these phenomena. That involves a critique of various forms of Nominalism. See my 1978a. Arguments against disjunctive and negative properties are developed in my 1978b, Chapter 14. It should be noted also that as the argument of this essay develops, a new and more relaxed sense of the word 'property' will be introduced, a sense in which a disjunction of universals or the negation of a universal can be said to be a property. But these relaxed properties are still not universals.

It seems, however, that a Principle of *Instantial Invariance* should be enforced on relations. For all numbers, n, if a relation is n-adic in one instantiation, then it is n-adic in all its instantiations. The rationale for this is straightforward enough. If one has, say, R*ab* and R*cde*, then it is hard to see how R could be *identical* in its different instantiations.[2] This does have the consequence that so-called anadic or multigrade relations, that is, relations which can take a different number of terms in different instantiations, are not genuine universals. Perhaps they are a more or less closely knit *family* of universals, with the predicate applying in virtue of just one or more members of the family.

Like the properties, although the relations are simple this does not rule out their having properties, and there being relations between relations. But for the present we do not consider the possibility of their having such higher-order properties and relations.

As in the case of properties, relations are not to be promiscuously postulated. For instance, there is no automatic inference from polyadic predicates to relations of that -adicity. What relations there are is, again, to be established *a posteriori* on the basis of scientific theory.

Properties and relations have been distinguished. But more or less under the inspiration of Russell, we can see properties as a mere limiting case among the universals. Properties are the monadic case. Relations are the dyadic, triadic, . . . n-adic cases, that is, the polyadic cases.

We have already suggested that point-instants are a candidate for individuals. As candidates for the relations, we have causal and spatio-temporal relations. Candidates for properties might be such things as charge and mass, non-relationally conceived. But, to re-emphasize, these examples should be thought of more as aids to the understanding than an attempt to advance a doctrine.

Individuals, properties and relations are brought together in

---

2 Perhaps the force of the Principle of Instantial Invariance can be brought out in the following way. Suppose that R*ab*, R*cde* and R*fg*, with R supposed to be the same relation in each case. Does not R in the second case lack *complete* resemblance, complete resemblance in its own intrinsic nature, to R in the first and third cases? But without complete resemblance, there is not identity.

Another argument is: Properties appear to be no more than the monadic case of universals. But if that is so, and if Instantial Invariance is denied, why not both R*ab* and R*c*, with R the same universal? This conclusion, however, seems very unintuitive.

what Wittgenstein called *facts* and what I shall call *states of affairs*. Once properties and relations have been introduced, the necessity for recognizing states of affairs should be clear. The existence of the individual a and the property F by no means ensures that a is F. If we are ontologically serious, we shall require a truth-maker to correspond to this truth: the state of affairs of a's being F.[3]

If a and F are simples, then we can call a's being F an *atomic* state of affairs. As emphasized in the *Tractatus*, each atomic state of affairs is logically independent of all the others. States of affairs that are independent of each other in this way may be called 'Hume independent'.

We shall speak of a and F as *constituents* of the state of affairs. It is clear that they are not *parts* of the state of affairs, in the sense of 'part' studied in mereology, the so-called calculus of individuals. If a exists and F exists, then their mereological sum, a + F, automatically exists. But as we have noted, the state of affairs of a's being F does not automatically exist. If a has R to b, and b has R to a, with R non-symmetrical, then we have two independent states of affairs. But the two states of affairs have exactly the same constituents. By contrast, there is just one sum of a, R and b. It is because non-simple properties and relations involve states of affairs (as we will see) that I speak of their constituents rather than their parts.

It is indeed vital to understand that states of affairs are non-mereological 'wholes'. Consider the relationship between a state of affairs, such as a's being F, and the two constituents of the state of affairs, a and F. The obtaining of the state of affairs entails the existence of the constituents, but the constituents could exist in the absence of that state of affairs. This might suggest a whole-part relation as studied by mereology. But if that suggestion were true, then the state of affairs would contain a surplus that would be a distinct existence from the constituents, and detachable from them. But there is no such extra 'factor' in the state of affairs.

It is well known to metaphysicians, at least since the time of

---

3 We could put Quine's famous test for ontological commitment by saying that he requires a truth-maker for the referential component of true statements but not for any other component. I hold that predicates also require truth-makers, although the semantic relations between predicates and universals differ from case to case. I have called Quine's stance on the predicate 'Ostrich nominalism' (see my 1978a, p. 16, and 1980; for dissent, see Devitt 1980 and Quine 1980). The deniers of states of affairs may also be described as ontological ostriches, although, of course, they need not be *Nominalists*.

F. H. Bradley, that there is no escape from a non-mereological mode of composition here by postulating a relation, R, that holds together a and F in the state of affairs. Now, a's having R to F again entails, but is not entailed by, the existence of the putative constituents, a, R and F.

It may be worth noting that this contrast between parts of individuals and constituents of states of affairs holds even if, contrary to the position taken in this essay, properties and relations are taken to be particulars rather than universals.[4] Suppose that a exists, the *particularized* asymmetrical relation R exists, and b exists. The sum $a + R + b$ automatically exists. No state of affairs involving these three constituents need exist. Suppose, however, that a state of affairs involving just these three constituents exists. It might be either a's having R to b, or b's having R to a. It appears that the recognition of properties and relations in an ontology, whether universals or particulars, leads to the recognition of states of affairs and so to the recognition of constituents of the states of affairs, constituents that are not in the mereological sense parts of the states of affairs.

Going back to a point of mere terminology, the choice between the phrases 'states of affairs' and 'facts' is a little delicate. 'Facts' may seem to have the advantage that there cannot be false facts, whereas language does seem to permit talk of non-existent states of affairs. But we shall see shortly that this apparent advantage is not really an advantage. It is in fact useful to have a relaxed sense of 'state of affairs' in which it is possible to talk of non-existent states of affairs.

A positive reason for not using the term 'fact' is our very strong tendency to speak of any true proposition as a fact, and of true propositions that are not logically equivalent as different facts. My (existent) states of affairs are truth-makers for propositions, where the one truth-maker may be the ontological ground for more than one true proposition. For instance, the state of affairs that a certain particular has a certain determinate shade of colour might make it true that the particular is scarlet, is red and is coloured.

We have now introduced states of affairs and have pointed out, without fully investigating, the special relation in which they stand

---

4 See, for instance, the views of G. F. Stout and D. C. Williams. I discuss such views in my 1978a, Ch. 8, and, more sympathetically, in *Universals* (1989).

to their constituents. This may suggest a tinker-toy picture in which states of affairs are built up from the constituents. But now I want to argue for a greatly enhanced position for that which the constituents constitute. The constituents are essentially aspects of, abstractions from, the states of affairs.

Consider the totality of atomic states of affairs. (The following formulation is indebted to Skyrms's 1981 article.) We may think of an individual, such as *a*, as no more than an *abstraction* from all those states of affairs in which *a* figures, F as an abstraction from all those states of affairs in which F figures, and similarly for relation R. By 'abstraction' is not meant that *a*, F and R are in any way other-worldly, still less 'mental' or unreal. What is meant is that, whereas by an act of selective attention they may be *considered* apart from the states of affairs in which they figure, they have no existence outside states of affairs.

Here is a way of conceiving of properties and relations which, if correct, makes clear the dependence of these 'entities' upon states of affairs (see Seargent 1985, Chapter 4). Properties are to be thought of as *ways that individuals are*. (If properties of properties are admitted, they will be further ways that ways are.) Relations are to be thought of as ways in which a certain number of individuals stand to each other. This conception of properties and relations makes it clear that there can be no uninstantiated properties and relations. A *possible* property or relation, even an empirically (nomically) possible property or relation, is not *ipso facto* a property or a relation.

Properties and relations thus depend on individuals, and are found only in states of affairs. What of individuals? Are they equally dependent on properties and relations? Not on relations. An individual which does not stand in any relations to other individuals (or, at any rate, external relations, which, it will subsequently be argued, are the prime candidates for our polyadic universals) seems to be a possibility. But could an individual be propertyless? Can it exist, but not in any particular way?

I do not think it can. An individual, to be an individual, must surely be *one* thing. But to be one must it not 'fall under a concept', as Frege would put it, that is to say, have some unit-making property? Without that, it is not even *an* individual. So I think we can reject bare individuals as well as uninstantiated properties and relations. States of affairs rule!

Before leaving this ontological sketch I will call attention to what may be called Ramsey's problem (1925).

The problem is this. What in this scheme marks off particulars from universals? It is customary to say that universals are ones which run through many. We have F*a* and F*b,* and again R*cd* and R*ef,* where F and R are such ones. All very well. But equally do we not have F*a*, G*a*, R*ab* . . . where now *a* is a one which runs through many? Ramsey concludes that there is no major distinction here. His opinion has recently been endorsed by Hugh Mellor (1980, pp. 123–4). It may have been Wittgenstein's view.

I have three answers to the Ramsey problem.

First, there is the answer of Aristotle. Primary substance is that of which things are predicated, but is not itself predicated of anything. Properties are properties *of* individuals. Relations are relations *holding between* individuals. But individuals are not individuals *of* their properties. Nor do individuals hold between the relations which relate them. So, at any rate, ordinary discourse assures us. It seems reasonable to take this asymmetry recognized by discourse as marking a rather fundamental ontological asymmetry.

Second, the theory of states of affairs developed in this section treats individuals and universals in a quite different fashion. Universals have a definite -adicity. They are monadic, dyadic . . . , an -adicity which, I argued, does not change from instantiation to instantiation. Given a universal, then the number of individuals it links in a token state of affairs is fixed. But given an individual, the -adicity of the universals that it instantiates is by no means fixed. The individual must, I think, instantiate at least one monadic universal. But after that it is on its own. What relations it has to other individuals, and what the -adicity of these relations is, is a contingent matter. So individuals and universals belong to different categories.

Third, I shall argue in Chapter 4 that there is (a) sense in which individuals are all the same. In abstraction from their properties and relations they are barely numerically different. (This is the rejection of the doctrine of *haecceity*.) By contrast, properties and relations do each have their own haecceity, or, better, their own quiddity or nature.

I conclude, then, against Ramsey, that the one that runs through the many where many individuals have the one property is not to be assimilated to the one that runs through the many where the one individual has many properties.

Once we have the notion of an atomic state of affairs, we can introduce the notion of a *molecular* state of affairs. Notice that here they are confined to *conjunctions* of states of affairs. (And, we may note in advance, they are supervenient on the existence of their conjuncts.) Molecular states of affairs do not involve negative or disjunctive states of affairs. There is, however, no bar to molecular states of affairs being infinite. If the world is in fact infinite (in time, say), then it will be a certain infinite conjunction of states of affairs.

We may now introduce the notion of a *possible* atomic state of affairs, and, in particular, a *merely possible* atomic state of affairs. The word 'possible' here modifies the sense of the phrase 'state of affairs'. For, as the phrase was introduced in Section II of this chapter, all states of affairs are actual.

The notion of a possible state of affairs is introduced semantically, by means of the notion of an atomic *statement*. Let *a* be a simple individual, and F and G two simple properties. Let *a* be F, but not G. Now consider the statements '*a* is F' and '*a* is G'. The former is true, and may be called an atomic statement. But the latter may *also* be called an atomic statement. While failing to correspond to an atomic state of affairs, it corresponds to the *form* of an atomic state of affairs: '*a*' picks out an actual atomic individual, 'G' falsely predicates a genuine simple property of this individual.

I pause here to note that no particular knowledge of what in fact these individuals and properties are is assumed. What we have here is a thought-experiment in which we imagine ourselves formulating a false atomic statement. In my view, Wittgenstein's avowal of ignorance here was a stroke of genius, and not, as is often thought, a cowardly evasion. It pays tribute to the fact that we have no *a priori* insight into, and even now only a little *a posteriori* insight into, the building-blocks of the world: the true individuals and the true universals. What does somewhat muddy Wittgenstein's insight is the thought that it should still be possible, by logical analysis alone, to get from *ordinary* true or false statements down to the atomic bedrock. This in turn is connected with the idea that necessities must one and all be analytic or tautological. Kripke has shown us the way ahead here. Some of his ideas about *a posteriori* (i.e. synthetic) necessities of identity will be incorporated into my argument as it advances.

Returning to the main line of the argument, 'a is G' is a false atomic statement. What it states, that a is G, is false. But we can also say that a's being G is a possible (merely possible) atomic state of affairs. I repeat what I have already said in Part I. A merely possible state of affairs does not exist, subsist or have any sort of being. It is no addition to our ontology. It is 'what is not'. It would not even be right to say that we can *refer* to it, at any rate if reference is taken to be a relation. Perhaps it is best to speak of *ostensible* reference. The parallel is with the ostensible (but very useful) reference that we make to ideal gasses, frictionless planes and so forth, in scientific investigations.

Instead of treating mere possibilities as non-existents, one could instead identify them with sets. For instance, the possibility that a is G could be identified with the set whose sole members are a and G. Whatever sets are, it is hard to deny that, given the existence of a and G, then this set exists. As a result, an Actualist can identify possibilities with something actual. As a matter of fact, Lycan (1979), who appears to have introduced the term 'Combinatorialism', takes it for granted that the Combinatorialist will adopt this approach (p. 305). The same assumption seems to be made by Lewis. In particular, Lewis interprets Skyrms's Combinatorial theory in this way, basing himself on the following text:

We may 'in the vulgar way', think of an atomic fact [in some world– DMA] as associated with a representation consisting of . . . an n-ary relation followed by n objects. (Skyrms 1981, p. 200)

Lewis interprets this passage as *identifying* possibilities with the 'representation', and so takes Skyrms's theory to be an *Ersatz* one.

However, Skyrms's phrase 'in the vulgar way' leaves his intentions ambiguous. And in correspondence he has told me that he is a Fictionalist rather than an *Ersatzer*. He takes mere possibilities to be non-existents. I think this is the right way to go. My reason is the simple one already advanced (Chapter 2, Section X). When we talk about possibilities we are talking about something represent*ed*, not a representation. (An ideal gas is not a representation.) Perhaps this argument will be dismissed as 'ordinary language'. But I think my view has a technical advantage as well. It seems that sets are supervenient on their members, that is, ultimately, things which are not sets. Supervenience, however, is a notion to be defined in terms of possible worlds, and hence in terms of possibility. It seems undesirable, therefore, to make use of sets in defining possibility.

So we take mere possibilities to be non-existents. Having introduced the notion of a possible atomic state of affairs, we can go on to introduce the notion of a possible molecular state of affairs. These are just conjunctions of possible atomic states of affairs, perhaps infinite conjunctions.

We have postulated here a stock, perhaps an infinite stock, of simple individuals, properties and relations, inextricably linked in states of affairs. It is at the heart of the matter that *any* statement involving these elements, and which respects the form of states of affairs (has the form 'Fa', 'Rab', '$Sabc$', etc.), states a possibility. So the possible atomic states of affairs are *all the combinations*. (The *merely* possible atomic states of affairs are the *re*combinations, the ones that do not exist.) In this way, the notion of possibility is given an analysis, an analysis which uses the universal quantifier. What remains to be seen is whether a plausible theory of properties and relations can be developed which permits this promiscuous recombination.

Now for possible worlds. The simplest way to specify a possible world would be to say that *any conjunction* of possible atomic states of affairs, including the unit conjunction, constitutes such a world. This is essentially correct, but three qualifications should be noted.

First, this suggestion would permit 'contracted' worlds, worlds which lack some of the simple individuals and/or simple properties and/or simple relations with which we started. As a matter of fact, we shall shortly admit such contracted worlds into our scheme. But certain complications are involved in doing so which it is desirable to postpone. So let us for the present restrict our conjunctions of possible atomic facts to those which at some point in the conjunction make use of *every* simple individual, property and relation involved in the *actual* world, involved, that is, in all the actual states of affairs.

Second, we need to eschew propertyless individuals. So an individual, *a,* say, must figure in at least one possible state of affairs of the form 'Fa'. The states of affairs it figures in cannot *all* be of the form 'Rab . . .' .

47

Third, even if these two constraints on molecular possible states of affairs are satisfied, what we have is not strictly a possible world. We have to make explicit a further condition: that this *is* the (supposed) totality of atomic states of affairs. But having taken notice of this potential problem, let us bracket it for the time being. Here, however, it may be noted that this totality condition will be used to provide truth-makers for negative statements. This is important because, as we will note in a moment, our scheme cannot admit negative states of affairs or negative universals.

Given these qualifications, then, any conjunction of possible atomic states of affairs constitutes a possible world. I will call these possible worlds the Wittgenstein worlds.

The possible atomic states of affairs are all the combinations of the simple individuals, properties and relations which respect the form of atomic states of affairs. The possible worlds are all the conjunctions of possible atomic states of affairs which respect the constraints discussed earlier. This, I take it, was Wittgenstein's inspiration (allowing that the details differ a little, in particular because Wittgenstein makes no use of universals, explicitly at least). The notion of possibility is analysed, reduced I think it can be said, to the combination of elements. Most of these combinations do not exist. They are the *mere* logical possibilities.

It remains to be seen whether the power and simplicity of this notion can carry it, or some suitable modification of it, through the difficulties which can be proposed.

One consequence of the view as so far developed is that we cannot admit negative states of affairs, or negative universals. Negative states of affairs were not stipulated in our construction. It is clear that they must be rejected. Suppose we try to admit both *a*'s being F and ~(*a*'s being F) as possible states of affairs. Our Combinatorial scheme would then allow us to select *both* these states of affairs for the one possible world, when in fact a 'world' containing both these possibilities is an impossible world.

If, however, we try to deal with the problem by introducing an extra constraint forbidding contradictory conjunctions in the one world, then we are using in our statement of constraints that very notion of modality which it was our hope to analyse. For contradictory states of affairs would be ones for which one state of affairs *must* obtain, and the other fail to obtain.

This, of course, faces us with a further task: that of providing a semantics for '$\sim(a$ is F)'. How does this contingent statement hook onto the world? It is rather easy to see how '(a is F) v (a is G)' hooks on. The truth-conditions are perspicuous. Not so with negation. The matter must be left aside for the present, but it will be dealt with in Chapter 7.

The situation is the same with negative properties and relations. If F is a property, then *not being F* is not a property, although there might be a genuine property with just that extension. If R is a relation, then *not being R* is not a relation. To admit both F and *not being F,* say, would be to ruin the Combinatorial scheme in just the way that negative states of affairs ruin it. In our Combinatorial scheme, *all simple properties and relations are compossible.*

IV FICTIONALISM

I have indicated my preference for a *Fictionalist* form of Combinatorialism as opposed to a more orthodox *Ersatz* version of the theory, a preference shared by Skyrms. I say that the (merely) possible worlds and possible states of affairs do not exist, although we can make ostensible or fictional reference to them. The *Ersatzer* identifies these entities with actually existing entities: suitable sets containing individuals and universals, if his building-blocks are the same as mine.

My quarrel with the *Ersatzer* is perhaps not very deep, and I should not be too distressed if I were forced back to his position. But the quarrel is real. Mere representations of possibilities, which is what the *Ersatzer* uses, are not to be identified with the possibilities that we seek to represent.

What account of fictional statements, then, should we accept? Not, clearly, an account in terms of possible worlds! But not only would such an account lead to circularity, it also ignores the fact that the notion of the fictional is linked to what is false, or nonexistent, but has no special link with possibilities. *Alice in Wonderland* and *Through the Looking Glass* are works of fiction. But some of the fictional situations that are described there are impossible. So are some of the situations portrayed in Escher drawings. Again, we might have the fiction that heat is not the motion of molecules. Yet if we accept Kripke's view of this proposition, as I think we should, it is an impossible fiction.

What is wanted, then, is an Actualist, one-world, account of fiction, and one that will accept both the merely possible and the impossible as fictions. I do not know in detail what account to give, but it would be truly surprising if no such satisfying account were available.

I used to think that, with modifications that are minor in this context, Lewis's multiverse taken as a fiction would serve. The trouble with this idea is that the fiction would be a fiction of a monstrously swollen actuality. But the merely possible worlds are *alternatives* to the actual world and to each other.

Picking up a suggestion that I have heard from Lewis (!), perhaps the matter can be handled this way. Each possible world is a different fiction about the way the world is. Logical space is the great fiction of a book of all these fictions: the book of worlds. We, of course, can only spell out a very small number of the individual fictions (ones that are very short). But we can indicate the general principles that determine just what there is in the book.

But, the Modal Realist may protest, must there not be some ontological gulf between the possible, even the merely possible, and the impossible? My answer to this is that making ostensible reference to the (merely) possible and, in particular, to the notion of (merely) possible worlds is, for certain philosophical and other purposes, a particularly useful thing to do. The usefulness springs from the fact that certain definite *constraints* have been put on such fictions. The constraints are somewhat less than the constraints that are put on useful scientific fictions such as ideal gasses, frictionless planes and economic men (constraints that would take some work to spell out). But there are definite constraints none the less. For instance, the general form of states of affairs must be respected, and possible worlds must answer to certain further restrictions which we will be spelling out. In speaking about the merely possible in ordinary discourse we have some informal or implicit sense of these restrictions. A Combinatorialist theory is meant to tell us just precisely what these restrictions are.

And it may well be an aid to the intellectual imagination, a creature which constantly needs the crutches of metaphor and make-believe, to treat mere possibilities as something real.

Of course, we want to say that (some) statements of mere possibility are *true*. I do not think this creates any difficulty. Some statements about ideal gasses, frictionless planes and economic men are true, while others are false. What is more, when statements about ideal gasses, frictionless planes and economic men are true, then they have truth-makers in the one and only real world. It may be tricky to spell out the exact way that such true statements correspond to the world, but surely it can be done.

If we compare 'p' and 'it is possible that p', what we can say in general is that we demand much less of the second statement than we do of the second in order to account it true. Nevertheless, we do make demands, demands which a theory of possibility, such as this essay, tries to spell out. These demands may be most simply and vividly formulated by a fictional device. We set up non-existent 'merely possible worlds' alongside the actual world, using certain principles, Combinatorial principles as I maintain. 'It is possible that p' is then said to be true if and only if a world can be found in which p is true. Like a true statement about ideal gasses, however, the truth-maker for 'it is possible that *p*' is to be found in *our* world.

V REJECTION OF ESSENTIALISM

One issue we should face immediately. It may be held that this particular Combinatorial account of possibility is too latitudinarian because it would permit anything to be of almost any nature. It would permit Bertrand Russell to be a poached egg, to adapt an example of Pavel Tichy's. Yet is this really a possibility?

Russell, of course, is not a simple individual. But we are at present assuming that he is made up of simple individuals. Could these individuals have had certain properties, certain relations to each other, and perhaps to other individuals having certain properties, such that the original individuals so propertied and related constitute a poached egg?

The difficulty really is to see why not. Perhaps Russell could not have been a poached egg if he has certain essential properties, properties which he has in all those possible worlds in which he exists. But it is notoriously difficult to give any principled reason for picking out a subset of his properties as essential. His humanity is the orthodox candidate. But once such a candidate is proposed, doubts can be raised. What is the difference between Russell's being some very stupid human being and being a dog, a jellyfish . . . or a poached egg? It seems to be a matter of the way it strikes one's imagination.

I do not think such doubts are in any way conclusive. But the

51

point is that it is so hard to give reasons on one side or the other of the debate whether Russell has any essential properties, that it seems reasonable to let the matter be decided elsewhere: by what seems to be on other grounds the best theory of possibility. It is a case of spoils to the victor.

Meanwhile, I think some explanation can be given, from the standpoint of an unrestricted Combinatorial theory, why certain possibilities seem so far-fetched. I shall begin by drawing the distinction between the *thin* and the *thick* particular.

The thin particular is what we have to this point spoken of as the individual. It is the particular in abstraction from all its properties and relations, the particular *qua* particular only. I have not spoken of it as the *bare* particular because that might suggest that it could exist in independence of any properties and relations. But although always clothed it is *thin*.

But we also think of the properties of particulars, and especially their non-relational properties, as *in some sense* part of the particular. As we will now see, states of affairs can accommodate the point.

The first point to notice is that states of affairs are particulars rather than universals. For *a*'s being F is no more susceptible of repetition than *a* is. The constituents of a state of affairs are particulars and universals, but what they make up is a particular. In my 1978a (Chapter 11, Section III) I called this 'the victory of particularity'. (It does something to help explain, without justifying, the appeal of Nominalism.)

Consider now the states of affairs involving a certain particular, but confine ourselves to the non-relational properties of that particular. Roll up all these properties into a conjunctive property. (Unlike disjunctive and negative properties, there seems to be no objection to conjunctive properties.) We can identify the state of affairs of that particular having that property as the *thick* particular. That property, and its conjuncts, are not parts of the particular in the orthodox mereological sense. But they are constituents of the state of affairs, and so in a sense they are parts of the particular.

Now, that the *thick* particular has a certain non-relational property is a necessary truth, for it is true in every possible world that contains that thick particular. (In general, however, it will not be an analytic truth, or one that is known *a priori*.)

Having introduced the notion of the thick as well as the thin particular (the individual), we can see that it is possible to work with particulars of intermediate thickness. In a rather vague and imprecise way, it seems that this is what ordinary thought and discourse do. When considering possibilities for Russell we are unlikely to take him merely as a thin particular, nor yet as a thick particular. What we do is to presuppose certain truths, or what we take to be truths, about Russell. The truth-makers for these will be certain states of affairs – a certain simple individual having certain properties and relations, including perhaps relations to further individuals. The possibilities which interest us concerning Russell keep these states of affairs constant. If they are not kept constant, then we will not be so inclined to say that the possibility is a possibility *about Russell*.

So it seems that it can be maintained with reasonable plausibility that the individuals (as opposed to their properties and relations) that constitute Russell could, collectively, have. properties that would make them a poached egg, although it might well be that we would not count this collection of particulars as *Russell's* being a poached egg. The essentialist alternative has its own implausible arbitrariness. As a result, we do not have here a particular reproach to (although equally no advantage for) a Combinatorialist scheme.

Perhaps, then, Combinatorialism can meet this first of the many challenges it must face.

4

Expanding and contracting the world

Suppose one is a *Naturalist,* holding that the space-time world is all there is. Suppose further that one holds that this space-time world has an ultimate structure: It is a conjunction of states of affairs whose constituents are individuals having (universal) properties and relations, the identification of these universals being an *a posteriori* matter. Suppose, finally, that one holds a *Combinatorial* theory of possibility, holding, in particular, that all *mere* possibilities are (non-existent) recombinations of actual elements.

Two difficulties present themselves: First, is it not possible that there should be universals which neither are identical with actual (that is, instantiated) universals nor have as constituents actual universals? Following Lewis (1986a, pp. 91–2), call such universals *alien* universals. Second, is it not possible that there should be individuals which are neither identical with actual individuals nor put together out of actual individuals? Call such individuals *alien* individuals. Alien universals and alien individuals seem to be ruled out by our three premises.

The present section will consider the question of alien universals. I will deny their possibility. The position concerning alien individuals is more complex. I am reluctant to deny their possibility. As a result, a modification of the Combinatorial scheme is forced on me. That will be a matter for a succeeding section; in the meanwhile we address the problem of alien universals.

Just to put the point aside permanently, let us be clear that 'being alien' is not an epistemological notion. Suppose that it is known that the world contains certain properties and relations, but it is not known that it contains any other ones. It is perfectly intelligible, and may be true (although in my view the 'may' is doxastic only), to say that there exist properties and relations which are totally alien relative to the known universals. Perhaps they are properties and relations of which we will never know anything. Such universals would not be alien in Lewis's sense. They would be actual and, as such, 'available' for recombination. Alien universals, however, as opposed to universals that are merely alien relative to the known universals, *do not exist*. Nevertheless, it may be argued, there might have been universals quite other than the ones which exist. ('Exist', of course, is being used to range over all times. Existence *now* is not the point.) The possibility of such universals, it seems, refutes our Combinatorialism.

I think that what the Combinatorialist must do is to take his courage in his hands and deny the possibility of alien universals. Skyrms, however, in his 1981 paper, denies that such strong measures are necessary. He says that here it is satisfactory to desert combination for 'analogy'. Analogy, as he explains it, turns out to be the use of the existential quantifier in a Ramsey sentence. Alien universals would be *like* the actual universals in being universals (that, I take it, is the 'analogy') but unlike them in being *other*. They cannot be named, no examples can be given, but the bare statement that such things exist states an unrealized possibility.

I do not think this treatment will serve. Suppose that it is said that actually existing individual *a* might have had an alien property. What makes this statement true? What is the truth-maker, or ontological ground? If alien properties are possible, then each of them will have its own nature – its *quiddity,* as we may put it. If it is true that *a* might have had an alien property, then equally *b* might have had another such property. But if this is a possibility, then is it not equally a possibility, and a different one, that *a* should have had the property *b* had, and *b* the property *a* had? Quiddities would be swapped. But where are these natures, these quiddities, to be found? A Platonist could give them uninstantiated existence 'alongside' the natural world, and they would then be available for recombination. Lewis can instantiate them in other possible worlds. But these moves are unavailable to the Naturalist-Combinatorialist. So what possibility is Skyrms pointing to?

Skyrms, we might say, is trying to use the determinable notion of nature-in-general, in place of the determinate notions of particular natures or quiddities. But that in fact focuses the difficulty. What is possible *could be*. Something merely determinable could not

55

be. To be is to be determinate. A possible property would have to have a determinate nature. But for the Naturalist, at least, the only determinate natures are those instantiated in the space-time world, or those which are recombinations of such natures.

It might be suggested that we use actual universals to 'triangulate' alien universals. The inspiration is Hume's 'missing shade of blue'. Consider the (putative) universals, redness, orange and yellow, and again red, purple, blue. Suppose orange never to have been instantiated. Would it not then have been alien? But, even so, could we not 'fix' it as the property which would lie between red and yellow, in the same way that purple actually lies between red and blue?

In criticism of this suggestion, the first point to notice is that the ploy is of limited value only. Orange would not be totally alien. After all, orange is a *colour*. By hypothesis, the *totally* alien could not be triangulated thus.

But in any case I doubt whether orange is in *any* degree alien relative to the other colours. If physicalist reduction of some sort gives the true nature of colour, as I believe to be the case, then the colours are different positions on a scale or scales of quantities. Quantities, in turn, are structural properties. A 'missing structure' is then combinatorially accessible from actual (i.e. instantiated) structures.

The strongest way to mobilize intuition in favour of alien universals is this (see Lewis 1986a, pp. 159–65). Anticipating the argument of the present chapter a little, consider a 'contracted' world, contracted by removing, say, certain simple properties from the actual world. From the standpoint of this contracted world, these simple properties will be alien properties. But if, relative to a contracted world, properties in our world could be alien, are there not possible worlds relative to which the actual world is contracted with respect to certain simple properties? Such worlds will contain universals alien to our world.

But this line of thought covertly depends on taking all possible worlds as equal. The Combinatoralist, however, is an actual-world chauvinist. The actual world, and it alone, is genuinely a world. The actual universals set a limit, a limit given by the totality of their recombinations, to the possible universals. The possible is determined by the actual, and so, saving recombination, cannot outrun the actual. Hence, to consider a contracted world is to suppose, falsely, that the actual world is contracted. With the actual supposed contracted, the possible will be supposed contracted, and certain actual universals supposed alien. But that does not licence *expanded* worlds.

This is relatively harsh doctrine. I do concede that, *offhand,* alien universals look to be a possibility. Nevertheless, this looking-to-be is no more than a philosopher's intuition. The possibility of alien universals is certainly not a piece of Moorean common sense, to be rejected at great intellectual peril. It can be rejected if it clashes with a theory of possibility which is attractive on a number of other solid grounds. Such a theory I take Combinatorialism to be.

But, in any case, we can go a good way towards explaining the intuition away. It must be allowed that alien universals are conceivable, that is, doxastically possible. Consider Goldbach's conjecture that every even number is the sum of two primes. It is conceivable, doxastically possible, that it is false. But a chain of mathematical reasoning may be discovered which proves that it is a necessary truth. Now, I have not proved the impossibility of alien universals, but it does appear that that impossibility follows from a certain theory of possibility. If that theory is true, then alien universals are impossible. But it is an intelligible thought that alien universals are possible, if only because nobody, at this stage of philosophical inquiry, can *know* that he puts forward a true theory of possibility.

Confusion between what is really possible, and what is merely conceived to be possible (i.e. is doxastically possible), a confusion still rife in our philosophical thinking, may then be appealed to as explaining, in part at least, the strength of the intuition in favour of the possibility of alien universals. Furthermore, as we shall see, Combinatorialism itself permits a plausible account of doxastic possibility. It is a matter of recombination of elements which are believed to be, or are not known not to be, distinct elements.

II MORE INDIVIDUALS

What then of alien *individuals?* Here the problem for the Combinatorialist is rather more severe. We have, with a little trepidation, denied the possibility of alien universals. But it seems very hard to deny that it is possible that the world should contain more individuals than it actually contains. There is no mouse in my study. Nevertheless, it is possible that there should be one. But why does this mouse have to be one of the world's mice? Why not an additional mouse? And, if additional, why not made up of particles (assume a materialist theory of mice) which are additional to the world's particles? The supposition is very much less *recherché* than the supposition of alien universals. It seems to be a genuine possibility. But how is the Combinatorialist to account for it?

I suggest that in the case of alien individuals Skyrms's appeal to 'analogy' can be upheld. It enables us to form the notion of an 'outer sphere' of possibility which, with respect to individuals, is not combinatorially formed. But, I shall also argue, in order to do this it is necessary to reject a doctrine that Skyrms apparently accepts for non-alien individuals: the doctrine of *haecceity*. So first a discussion of this doctrine.

Let us use as an example a contracted world which contains nothing but the simple individuals *a* and *b*, along with the properties F and G, which are also simple. Assume that this world is exhausted by the states of affairs:

I   Fa & Gb

What will the Combinatorialist say are the merely possible worlds relative to an actuality thus thinly conceived? For simplicity's sake let us ignore contractions: worlds without one or more of F or G or *a* or *b*. *Prima facie,* we then have:

II   Ga & Fb
III Fa & Ga & Fb
IV   Fa & Fb & Gb
V   Fa & Ga & Gb
VI   Ga & Fb & Gb
VII Fa & Ga & Fb & Gb

Consider now the pairs I and II, III and IV, and V and VI. Carnap would say that, although the members of each pair have different *state-descriptions,* they have the same *structure-description* (1962, Chapter III, Sections 18, 27)'. In the case of III and IV, for instance, the structure-description is: one simple individual having the simple properties F and G, the other having F alone. The question is: are I and II, III and IV, V and VI the very same world, or are they different worlds?

Here we find the dividing line between Haecceitism and anti-Haecceitism. The Haecceitist holds that the members of each pair differ from each other. The anti-Haecceitist denies it. This has a consequence for Combinatorialism. The anti-Haecceitist Combinatorialist will countenance *fewer possible worlds* than the Haecceitist does. For the anti-Haecceitist I = II, III = IV, and V = VI. From his point of view there is something a bit misleading about a symbolism such as 'F*a* & G*b*' to represent a world, because it insinuates that there is another world symbolizable by 'G*a* & F*b*'. For the anti-Haecceitist the situation is better described as being that of a world containing just two individuals, one of which has the simple property F while the other has the simple property G.

The Haecceitist, however, holds that *a* and *b* each have a unique inner essence, a metaphysical signature tune as it were, something apart from their repeatable properties F and G, which distinguishes them. Even abstracting from their repeatable properties, *a* and *b* differ *in nature*. So for the Haecceitist each member of the pairs is distinct from the other member.

Notice that there could be a *strong* and a *weak* form of anti-Haecceitism. A strong anti-Haecceitist denies that individuals are anything more than the 'bundles' of their properties. For the strong anti-Haecceitist world VII collapses into a one-individual world, an individual having the properties F and G. For each of the 'two' bundles contains the very same properties united by the very same nexus. The weak anti-Haecceitist does not collapse world VII into a single individual world. He does not analyse individuality in terms of universals. As a result, he allows possible worlds where two or more individuals instantiate the very same universals, worlds which do not insist on the Identity of Indiscernibles, the Dissimilarity of the Diverse.

I reject strong anti-Haecceitism, the 'bundle of universals' view of individuals, for reasons which I have given elsewhere (1978a, Chapter 9) and will not repeat here. Here, then, the choice lies between Haecceitism and weak anti-Haecceitism.

Haecceitism for individuals is parallel to Quidditism for universals. Quidditism for universals seems very plausible. Each universal must surely have its own nature. When this simple thought is linked with a Naturalist Combinatorialism, however, it makes alien universals impossible. Equally, however, Haecceitism, when linked with a Naturalist Combinatorialist theory of possibility, makes alien individuals impossible. For the alien individual, wholly other than actual individuals, must be supposed to have some definite haecceity, different from, and not obtainable combinatorially from, actual haecceities. But how can a Naturalist provide a truth-maker for statements about the possibility of alien individuals, with their alien haecceities? It seems that he cannot.

But the rub is that, although we can with reasonable plausibility deny the possibility of alien universals, alien individuals seem straightforwardly possible. Remember the alien mouse in my study.

Skyrms would once again appeal to 'analogy', to the existential quantifier. Alien individuals, individuals quite other than those which exist, are a possibility because we can assert that they might exist without attributing to them any definite haecceity. But if what is possible could be, and to be is to be definite, determinate, and if individuals have a haecceity, then the alien individuals must be conceived to have *some* definite haecceity, and one other than any haecceity of actual individuals. But for a Naturalist like Skyrms, there is nothing to play the role of such a haecceity.

I suggest, therefore, that the Naturalist-Combinatorialist should move to the weak anti-Haecceitist position. I think it is quite a natural and comfortable view. And then, I hope, we can revive the Skyrms doctrine of 'analogy' in more favourable circumstances.

The idea is quite simple. If weak anti-Haecceitism is true, then individuals *qua* individuals (abstracting, that is, from their proper-ties and relations) are merely, barely, numerically different from each other. They are *simply* other. In this they are unlike properties and relations. This concept of otherness is derivable from actuals. When applied to further, alien, individuals, it encompasses the whole of their nature *qua* individuals. Nothing is missing, as it would be missing if Haecceitism were true. So we can form a *fully determinate* concept of an indefinite number of alien individuals 'by analogy'. They are then available to form worlds additional to the Wittgenstein worlds.

Let us not conceal that this manoeuvre does involve a qualifica-tion of, a moving away from, Combinatorialism. Our alien indi-viduals are reached not combinatorially but, rather, conceptually, 'by analogy'. But I suggest that it is a minor and acceptable qualification.

One matter remains. Is there any difficulty for the weak anti-Haecceitist in identifying individuals across possible worlds? For the Haecceitist there is no difficulty at all. There is the same haec-ceity, if perhaps a difference in properties or relations. But if worlds which 'exchange' individuals without difference in the property-and-relation structure of the world are *not* different worlds, how can we identify individuals in different worlds? Or do we have to retreat to mere counterparts?

I think the answer is that, provided we start with individuals in the *actual* world, then there is no objection to thinking falsely of *them* as having properties or relations they do not have. That, after all, is the foundation of the Combinatorial idea. It yields us (mere) possibilities and (merely) possible worlds in which they figure. (Notice, by the way, that Haecceit*ism* is sometimes taken to be simply the doctrine that individuals can be genuinely identical across worlds. So I could perhaps be said to be upholding a form of Haecceit*ism,* although rejecting haecceit*ies.*)

But how then do we 'decide' whether an individual in a merely possible world, which perhaps is very *like* an individual in the actual world, is or is not identical with the actual individual? I think Kripke's answer is on the right track here (1980, p. 44). We stipulate that there is an identity. We have, as we take it, managed to *refer* to some individual in the world. *It,* then, is 'available for recombination'. We refer to that thing, verbally or mentally, but go on to suppose of that thing something we take to be false. Provided the supposition obeys certain minimal constraints, the ones that we are trying to spell out, what we have is a *possibility* for that individual.

III CONTRACTED WORLDS

So the Wittgenstein worlds require to be supplemented by worlds which contain alien individuals, but not by worlds which contain alien universals.

But there is more to be done. Not only must we allow this limited expansion, but we must also countenance contraction. If there is no contraction, then every actual individual, and every simple universal, will appear in every possible world. As has often been noted, that would make both the individuals and the universals necessary beings. It is natural, however, to think that they are *contingent* beings. Of any individual in the natural world, it seems true to say that it might not have existed. Of any universal in the actual world, it seems true to say that it might not have been instantiated (at any time). This means for our Naturalism that the universal might not have existed.

The obvious solution is to allow contraction in the forming of possible worlds. Any given individual is contingent. That is, there are worlds which omit this individual. Any given universal is contingent. That is, there are worlds which omit this universal. Such contraction does not seem unreasonable. Why, one may ask, in combining elements into states of affairs, and then conjoining these states of affairs to make possible worlds, are we forced to make use of *every* actual and simple individual, property and relation? Why not a proper subset?

There is, however, a matter which deserves consideration. There seems to be no particular difficulty about the contraction of *individuals*. But contraction of universals does raise problems for Combinatorialism. The difficulty was pointed out by W. G. Lycan (1979, pp. 306–7), citing Philip Quinn.

As the modal logicians say, the Wittgenstein worlds are all 'accessible' to each other; that is, each of them is a possible world *relative to any other*. In this respect, they form an equivalence class. The relation of accessibility is reflexive, transitive and symmetrical, and so is governed by an S5 modal logic. Given our anti-Haecceitist account of individuals, it seems that the situation does not change if worlds are added which add and/or subtract individuals.

But suppose that we consider a contracted world, W_c, contracted by the absence of the simple property F, relative to a Wittgenstein world, W_w, which contains Fs. W_c is accessible from W_w, that is, is a possible world relative to W_w. Given Combinatorial theory, however, W_w is not accessible from W_c. This is because, relative to W_c, F is an alien property. Given our stand on alien universals, symmetry of accessibility then fails. For a set of worlds which contains both W_w and W_c one must content oneself with an *S4* modal logic. (Accessibility becomes reflexive and transitive, but not symmetrical.)

This, indeed, is the formal analogue of points made in Section I of this chapter, where we considered Lewis's argument that other possible worlds contain universals that are alien to this, the actual world. We met Lewis's argument by simple denial. If one accepts Lewis's form of Modal Realism, with all possible worlds equal and 'actuality' an indexical term, then the case for alien universals seems overwhelming. But if one is an Actualist, a this-world chauvinist, then it seems reasonable to deny the possibility of alien universals, particularly after drawing a sharp distinction between the possible and the conceivable.

But although we do not want to allow the expansion of universals (except combinatorially), we do want to permit their contraction. How can it be denied that a certain simple universal might not have been instantiated? But to make such a supposition is to suppose actuality contracted, and then, with this supposition made, actual actuality will contain a universal alien to the supposed actuality. Hence the actual world becomes inaccessible to, that is, not a possible world relative to, the supposed world. But this, we argued, a Combinatorialist can accept. You cannot get the actual world combinatorially from the supposed world. With actuality contracted, possible worlds must be considered contracted. That seems straightforward. Its formal expression is that a class of worlds which contains both the actual world and certain contracted worlds must have an S4 rather than an S5 logic.

So Quinn's point is noted and accepted.

In this section we have been thinking of contraction as involving the removal from a world of individuals, properties or relations. It is to be noted, however, that there is what might be called a minor mode of contraction. In the minor mode no individuals, properties or relations are obliterated, but only states of affairs. If what we start out with is the actual world, then this minor sort of contraction does not take us outside the class of Wittgenstein worlds.

Of any two states of affairs whatever, atomic or not, which are found together in a world, then, if either can be removed without removing the other, they are, in a phrase already introduced, 'Hume distinct' (see Chapter 3, Section II). Distinct *atomic* states of affairs are automatically Hume distinct.

IV REJECTION OF THE EMPTY WORLD

There is, however, an ultimate contraction which a Combinatorial theory cannot accept. It cannot countenance the empty world. For the empty world is not a construction from our given elements (actual individuals, properties and relations). For the Combinatorialist, then, it is necessary that there be something. Of course there is no particular something which it is necessary that there be. But the smallest possible world will be a state of affairs of the form F*a*, with F and *a* simple.

I have already argued in Chapter 2, Section VI, that there is no particular paradox in this. Philosophers are inclined to say, offhand, that there could have been nothing at all. But this is only to follow out a relatively superficial line of reasoning. They can see no reason to prevent them proceeding from the distributive contingency of everything to the collective contingency of everything. But if an otherwise good theory blocks that inference, then so be it. The decision on whether the empty universe is or is not possible is, and should be, spoils for the victor.

The empty world is perhaps best thought of as an unreachable or ideal limit in the series of contracted possible worlds. We start with the actual world and subtract more and more elements from it, so allowing combinatorially for sets of possible worlds which are successively more and more impoverished. The paths down to these impoverished worlds could be very various. But all paths have the same limit: the empty world. As is the case with some limits, however, the limit is never reached.

It may be noted also that if we did admit the empty world then we should have to say that no other world was accessible from it. (They would contain alien universals.) From the standpoint of the empty world, it is a necessary being! This seems an additional good reason for a Combinatorialist to deny the possibility of the empty world.

V   A PICTURE OF THE SITUATION

We have not done with modifying our theory. We need to generalize it still further to allow for the possibility (at least doxastic) that the world fails to resolve itself into simple elements. We also need to provide for higher-order entities (higher-order properties, relations and states of affairs). But before doing so, it may be helpful to pause here in order to offer a pictorial model of the positive conclusions so far arrived at.

Picture then an indefinitely large peg-board, which itself pictures nothing. Into this board are stuck an indefinite number of identical hooks. These are the *actual individuals*. There are also available an indefinite further number of these hooks. These further hooks, if and when they are added to the board, represent merely possible individuals, individuals additional to the actual individuals. But all hooks are *completely interchangeable*. Merely to swap two hooks around, or to substitute one of the reserve hooks for a hook actually on the board, does nothing. It represents no ontological difference. This, of course, is the rejection of haecceities.

Each hook on the board must be hung with at least one coloured counter. The counters are the simple properties. Sameness of colour represents sameness of property. A hook hung with a counter is the simplest (i.e. monadic) atomic state of affairs. There is an indefinite reserve supply of counters of all colours for the representing of merely possible states of affairs. Only the colours present on the board are to be found in the reserve, however. This is the rejection of the possibility of alien properties.

Between some *n*-tuples of hooks there stretch linking strings of various colours. These represent simple relations, a different colour for each different relation. Hooks linked by such a string constitute *polyadic* states of affairs. The number of hooks connected by a string gives the *n*-adicity of the relation. A string of a certain colour always connects the same number of hooks (Instantial Invariance). Besides the actually used strings, there is available for putting on the board an indefinite supply for each colour of pieces of string. Every colour of string is present on the board: the rejection of alien relations.

If we consider the hooks, counters and strings actually on the board, giving us the actual world, then all their recombinations within the rules laid down, but where all hooks, and each counter and string *type* is used, give us the Wittgenstein worlds. Use of more hooks will give us the expanded worlds. Contracted worlds can be modelled by using fewer hooks or using fewer *types* of counter or string. There is a minor mode of contraction where only *tokens* of counters or strings are removed. This models the removing of atomic states of affairs from a world without removing any of the basic stock of individuals, properties and relations.

5

Relative atoms

I WHAT IF THERE ARE NO ATOMS?

The Combinatorial scheme as so far developed postulates simples: simple individuals, simple properties and simple relations, all conceived of as abstractions from atomic states of affairs. But is the world made up of simples in this way?

May it not be that some, or all, individuals have proper parts which in turn have proper parts, *ad infinitum?* It is not certain that, just by itself, this supposition contradicts the idea that the individuals concerned are not made up of simples. For one might hold that such individuals are made up of an infinite number of simple individuals. For instance, there are those who hold that any extension is infinitely divisible into extensions, and yet that extensions are made up of continuum-many simple points. However, we can sophisticate our question to allow for this complication. Might it not be that some, or all, individuals have proper parts which in turn have proper parts, *ad infinitum,* without there being simple constituents even at infinity?

Similar questions can be raised about properties and relations.

It might be, for instance, that the property F is nothing but the conjunction of two wholly distinct properties G and H, that G and H, in their turn, are conjunctions of properties, and so *ad infinitum.* This progression, it may be, does not even end 'at infinity'. There are no simple properties involved, even at the end of an infinite road.

Or, again, it may be that the property F dissolves into a *structure.* Perhaps to be an F is to be something with two disjoint parts: a G-part standing in relation R to an H-part. Perhaps to be a G is to be something with two disjoint parts: a J-part standing in relation S to a K-part. To be an H may dissolve into an L standing in relation T to an M. And so on forever. Structures all the way down, and no escape even at infinity.

The same may be true of some, or all, relations. For R to hold may be a matter of S & T both holding. S & T may dissolve similarly, with simple relations never reached.

It is a *contingent* matter whether a certain individual, property or relation is, or is not, indefinitely complex in the way described? In my 1978b (Chapter 15, Section I, and Chapter 18, Section II) I said this about properties and relations. But I now think this was a bad mistake. I am not sure what to say about individuals, so will leave them aside here. But that a certain universal is or is not simple now seems to me to be a necessary truth. Certainly, it may be a question to be decided *a posteriori* to the extent that it can be decided. But it is not a contingent matter. It is what we might call a Kripkean necessity.

Here is the simple *reductio ad absurdum* argument for this new position. Suppose that it is contingent whether property F is simple or not. There will then be a possible world where F exists (is instantiated, presumably) and is simple. There will be another possible world where F will be identical with, say, the conjunction G&H. But this seems absurd. What *identity* across possible worlds do we have here? Simple F in W_1 is identical with G&H in W_2? Why not with any other universal, simple, conjunctive or structural?

Here is what seems the best that one can do for the contingency view. In the actual world, say, a certain class of individuals has the simple property F. Properties G and H are not instantiated in this world. (In order to avoid difficulties about alien properties, let both G and H be complex properties.) In a certain possible world, the individuals that are F in the actual world (or their counterparts, if you prefer) lack F but do have G&H. The worlds do not differ in any further way except for the truths that supervene on this difference. (For example, the G&H world has a G-alone world as an accessible contraction, but the F-world has nothing corresponding.)

We may say that F in our world and G&H in another world play exactly the same role. This is to extend to *causal* role. Possession of F in this world and of G&H in the other has just the same causes and just the same effects, including effects on perceivers and, more generally, minds.

F in this world and G&H in the other are set in exactly the same environment. But can we say that F *is* G&H? I still do not see how we can. They may be said to be identical for all practical purposes. But I do not see how a philosopher, at least, could say that they are really identical. At best, each is a sort of counterpart of the other.

I conclude that we do have a necessity here. The further conclusion to be drawn is that if there are simple universals, or if the ultimate universals are *all* simple, then this is a matter of necessity. Similarly, if some or all universals involve no simple elements at any point, then this too is a matter of necessity. The structure, or make-up, of a universal cannot change from one possible world to another. (Universals, however, might have different *properties* and *relations* in different possible worlds. See Chapter 7.)

It seems clear that this sort of necessity will in many cases be a synthetic necessity, and discovered, if it is discovered, *a posteriori*. For instance, a certain property may have a certain effect on our senses. It may then be a matter for empirical investigation what the structure of this property is, if any. Characteristically, then, these necessities will be Kripkean necessities. Indeed, I suggest that this question of the structure of universals yields the theoretically clearest case of synthetic *a posteriori* necessities. Here I would favourably contrast these cases with the alleged Kripkean necessities concerning the necessities of origin for things. If we hold that anything that endures through time *ipso facto* has temporal parts – a view which is at least thoroughly natural for a Combinatorialist – then such a particular is a complex of shorter-lived particulars. By Combinatorialism, then, it can have a different origin from the one it actually has. And since the *independent* grounds adduced for accepting such necessities are by no means overwhelming, it seems reasonable to argue from Combinatorialism to the rejection of necessities of origin.

Again, it has been alleged by Kripke that, for instance, a certain lectern made of wood could not have been made of something else, such as ice. A Combinatorialist cannot accept this as a necessity either, on the Combinatorial grounds that an individual (a thin particular) may have any properties whatever. Although the Combinatorialist position here may not be obviously true, yet neither is Kripke's view. It seems reasonable to decide the matter on other grounds.

These points, however, though important to the argument of this essay as a whole, are tangential to our immediate purpose. It is granted that each universal may reduce to simple constituents, and granted that, if this is true, it is a necessary truth about each universal. Nevertheless, it surely remains *doxastically* open, a matter to be decided by natural science if decided at all, whether or not the world reduces to genuinely atomic states of affairs. So our theory of possibility had better be equipped to deal with the doxastic possibility that there are no atomic individuals, properties or relations.

We may so equip our theory, and, as we shall see, gain other advantages as well, by introducing the notion of *relative atoms*. Let the states of affairs which make up the world involve certain individuals, properties and relations. They may or may not be simple (doxastic 'may'). The totality of recombinations of these 'atoms' yields a set of possible worlds, which can be 'expanded' and 'contracted' in the usual way. If the atoms are genuine atoms, then no more remains to be done. But if the atoms are not genuinely atomic, then this set is a mere subset of the worlds which can be formed. With one or more of the 'atoms' broken up, we can go on to an enlarged set of worlds. If the breaking-up goes on forever, and reaches no genuine atoms even at infinity, then at each point in the break-up new worlds emerge. (And, incidentally, worries that atoms will appear in every possible world, and so be necessary beings, automatically evaporate.)

This may seem easy enough. But there is a vital condition to be placed on these relative atoms, a condition which complicates matters somewhat, although, as we shall see, it also opens up interesting prospects. This vital condition is automatically satisfied for the genuine atoms which we have been considering up to this point. The relative atoms – the individuals, the properties, the relations – must not merely be distinct (different) from one another but must be *wholly* distinct. Only if the relative atoms are wholly distinct from each other will *each* different recombination of atoms yield a different possible world.

In the case of individuals, the requirement of complete distinctness is simple enough to appreciate. It is just the mereological requirement that none of the individuals involved be, or contain, any part of another. If the putative relative atoms a and b overlap, partially or totally, then there will be a redundancy in worlds to which both a and b are assigned. This will be a cause of particular embarrassment if we then go on to consider worlds which contain a but in which b is totally absent, or which contain b and in which a is totally absent. These will be impossible worlds. But suppose it is not known that *a* and *b* overlap. We may wrongly take a world with Hesperus but not Phosphorus, or Phosphorus but not Hesperus, to be a possible world.

In the case of universals the requirement of complete distinctness of relative atoms is just as absolute, but the distinctness involved is not of the sort envisaged by the mereological calculus. The relative atoms involved will be either *conjunctive* or *structural* universals (where 'universals' covers both properties and relations). Disjunctive and negative properties and relations, although we shall later admit them in a subordinate capacity, are not admitted into the construction of the possible worlds.

Here I have to confess to another major and long-continued error. In my 1978b (Chapter 15, Section II) I considered the relation of the conjunctive property-universal *P&Q* to its conjunct P. I suggested the relation here was mereological: that it was exactly parallel to the relation, say, between Australia and the state of New South Wales. This cannot be right, or at any rate it cannot be right if it is combined with something that I am not at all willing to give up: the Principle of Instantiation for universals. Applied to the present case this principle demands that there exist some individual (past, present or future) such that it is both P and Q. Given this, the parallel with mereology (and so with individuals) fails. If individual *a* and *b* both exist, then, it is fundamental to mereology, an individual *a* + *b* also exists. But if monadic universals P and Q both exist, then although P + Q exists, it by no means follows that the universal *P&Q* exists. For there might be nothing that is both P and Q.

The fact is that *complex* universals (and merely relative atoms will have to be complex) involve *states of affairs*. I argued in Chapter 3 that universals only exist *embedded* in states of affairs – that is the Principle of Instantiation. But unlike simple universals (if there are any), complex universals themselves *embed* states of affairs. Suppose P and Q to be simple. They do not embed any state of affairs. But if the universal *P&Q* exists, there must be a complex state of affairs where some individual has P and that very same individual has Q. To articulate the nature of the universal involves reference to this state of affairs. This is what I mean by saying that *P&Q* embeds a state of affairs.

At this point we can understand why distinct complex universals do not stand in mereological relations to each other. For we have already seen (Chapter 3, Section II) that states of affairs do not stand to their constituents in mere mereological relations.

Nevertheless, states of affairs do have constituents. And it seems reasonable to extend the notion of constituents to complex universals, speaking, for instance, of P and Q as the constituents of the conjunctive universal *P&Q*. Or suppose that *a* has property F, *b*, which is wholly distinct from *a*, has F, and *a* has R to *b*. The complex individual [*a* + *b*] has a structural property which we may diagram as F-R-F. Suppose F and R to be simples. Then the ultimate constituents of this property are simply F and R, the very same as the ultimate constituents of a more complex property which can be diagrammed as F-R-F-R-F.

We can now give a straightforward formula for the condition for relative combinatorial atoms among universals when possible worlds are in question. For individuals, the relative atoms lack any common parts. For universals, the relative atoms lack common constituents.

There is no doubt that this condition for relative atoms is, for a Combinatorialist, a sufficient condition. There is a question whether it is a necessary condition, and, if not, what more tolerant conditions should be substituted. But I do not think that we need spend time on this problem. The point of introducing relative atoms is to deal with the doxastic possibility that at least some individuals, properties and relations cannot be decomposed into even an infinity of atoms. If this possibility is actual, then the (real) possibilities for the world can be encompassed only if each set of 'atoms' is dissolved to yield new possibilities by recombination. That being so, any scheme for relative atoms can be accepted which captures all these possibilities. The provision that in the case of universals relative atoms should lack common constituents appears to do this in a straightforward way.

II EPISTEMOLOGICAL INTERLUDE

Interesting consequences flow from the demand that relative atoms be wholly distinct or, more accurately, from this demand together with its being flouted *unaware*. To prepare for this, it will be useful to attend to some epistemological possibilities.

Suppose, first, that certain objects have the two properties P and Q which lack any common constituents. In virtue of these two properties, but working along two distinct channels correlated with the properties, the objects are able to stimulate the sense-organs of human perceivers. However, these two distinct channels meet, at a relatively low level of neurophysiological processing, at what we can think of as an *and* neuron. If this neuron receives a combination of a P-impulse and a Q-impulse, then, and only then, it fires, sending a single message to the higher command.

What will be the result of this? What presumably will happen is that a *complex* property, the conjunctive *P&Q*, will register in a simple way in the mind. In the case given, the perceiver has no resources for sorting out P and Q. A complex quality will register as something simple. Given only a little more detail in the story, the property involved could be a structural property, yet still register as a simple, unstructured, property.

Now let us have an *or* neuron. This may be stimulated by Ps alone, or Qs alone (or both). In all cases, it simply fires. Here, two properties which are different will register as if they are the same. The mind will overlook differences between properties.

Suppose, finally, that we have a *not* neuron.[1] We again require objects which are both P and Q, but now also other objects that are P but not-Q. If an object is both P and Q, then both the P-channel and the Q-channel fire. The Q-channel is inhibitory, however. As a result, the neuron fails to react. If, however, the object is P and not-Q then the P-channel fires but the Q-channel fails to fire. Lacking inhibition, the *not* neuron then fires, passing a message up the line.

What is the neuron reacting to in the second type of case? Not just to the presence of property P. It is reacting to (P&not-Q)s. And it is doing so even if we assume, as I do, that there is no universal *not being Q* and so no universal *P&not-Q*. What is more, the neuron is reacting, when it does fire, no differently than it would if it were built to react to P *simpliciter*. It still sends a simple message up the line. As far as the neuron is concerned, and so perhaps the perceiving mind, what it is reacting to is a simple property.

Given these basic cases, more complex cases can easily be conceived.

These examples cast a good deal of light on the contention of the *a posteriori* realist about universals that there is no simple rela-

---

1 This is a sophisticated *not* neuron. David Lewis pointed out to me that there could be a purer case: a neuron that fired if and only if it was not stimulated.

tionship between predicates, monadic and polyadic, and universals, monadic and polyadic. The 'manifest image' of the natural kinds may have to give way to a deeper classification: the 'scientific image' of the natural kinds.

But, more immediate to our present purposes, the leeway that such examples allow for universals that are not wholly distinct, but which we treat as if they *are* wholly distinct, allows us to make more clear the very important distinction between the conceivable and the possible. This is matter for the next section.

III DOXASTICALLY POSSIBLE WORLDS

Suppose that there is a set of individuals which have the conjunctive property *F&G,* a wholly distinct set which have *G&H,* and a third wholly distinct set which have *F&H.* Suppose, however, that these properties present themselves to us, say in perception, *via an and* neuron, as different, but unanalysed and so, for all we know, simple properties. Suppose that we give them the names 'A', 'B', and 'C'. Taking A, B and C as atoms, as we might feel entitled to do, we can form a set of possible properties [A, B, C, AB, AC, BC, ABC] which individuals might have. Clearly, these properties are not *wholly distinct*. But recombination has apparently given us seven *distinct* properties.

But suppose that we now feed in the (previously supposed unknown) analysis of A, B and C. Substituting in our set of possible properties we get [FG, GH, FH, FGH, FGH, FGH, FGH]. The last four terms are identical. Whatever we might have thought before being given the *constitution* of A, B and C, recombination in fact yields only *four* distinct properties.

Nevertheless, given that we cannot analyse properties A, B and C into their constituents, will we not naturally form the idea of seven distinct combinations? If they are then used in the formation of worlds, we get worlds which are epistemically distinct, or, better, doxastically distinct, but which are *not in fact distinct*. These worlds are not a subset of the possible worlds. The possible worlds are a subset of them.

We turn our attention now to cases involving a *not* neuron. Suppose that a neuron fires if stimulated by a P-channel but is inhibited from firing if stimulated simultaneously by a Q channel. It is in effect reacting to a P that is not a Q. But the reaction may be a simple affair, carrying no information about the relative complexity of the stimulus. Suppose further that another neuron fires if stimulated by a Q-channel, except when inhibited by a P-channel. The reaction here is to a Q that is not a P. Let this reaction, too, be a simple affair. The result might be the perception of two 'qualities', A and B, which in perception appear to be simple qualities. It might seem that they are available for combination, that there can be individuals in some possible world which are both A and B. In fact, however, this is an impossible world.

What this may yield us is a definition of a doxastically possible world. In a possible world, the elements from which it is constructed (individuals, properties, relations) are all wholly distinct. In a doxastically possible world, by contrast, the elements *are thought to be* or are *not known not to be* wholly distinct. Two doxastically possible states of affairs may be the very same possible state of affairs, and a doxastically possible state of affairs may not be a possible state of affairs.

Let us assume with Kripke, correctly in my view, that it is a necessary truth that heat is motion of molecules. It is nevertheless conceivable that heat is not motion of molecules; so there will be doxastically possible worlds where something is hot, but its molecules do not move, and other worlds where something's molecules move, but it is not hot. Notice, however, that if this case is to fit the definition, we do need to take 'is thought to be' in a way that abstracts from belief.

An interesting case to consider is that of alien universals, properties or relations quite other than those actually instantiated. They are conceivable. Some philosophers, Lewis in particular, have conceived of them. I have argued, however, that they are not *possible*. Because they are quite other, they are wholly distinct from the instantiated universals. So they fit smoothly into the suggested account of doxastically possible worlds. There are doxastically possible worlds containing alien universals, but all such worlds are, if I am right, impossible worlds.

But a more familiar sort of conceivability, conceivability in mathematics, may be more troublesome. Consider the proposition that the series of pair-primes (primes separated by 2) is infinite. It is conceivable that this is true, and conceivable that this is false. Nobody yet knows. This appears to be about a very strange individual: *the series of pair-primes.* A property, *being finite,* may or may not attach to it. How is this to be integrated into a theory of doxastically possible worlds?

I think that probably the trick can be worked. To do it I require a certain doctrine from the philosophy of mathematics, one I shall discuss in Chapter 9. It is a not uncommon view that the existence of a mathematical entity amounts to no more than the instantiation of that entity *in some possible world*.

Consider now the largest known pair-prime. (It might be known that larger pair-primes exist while not knowing just what these numbers are. Assume, for simplicity, that this is not the case.) This ensures the existence of a possible world containing N individuals, where N is the larger number of the pair. Now form the conception of an infinite series of doxastically possible worlds. The first of these contains at least N' individuals, where N' is a prime, $N'-2$ is a prime, and there is no pair-prime between $\{N-2, N\}$ and $\{N'-2, N'\}$. The next doxastically possible world in the series catches the next pair-prime, and so *ad infinitum*.

If the series of pair-primes has no termination, like the primes, then each of these doxastically possible worlds is also a possible world. If there is a greatest pair-prime, then the series begins with a certain number of doxastically possible worlds that are also possible worlds. After that point they are *merely* doxastically possible worlds.

I do not claim to have taken the matter very far. But there do seem to be quite good prospects for a theory of doxastically possible worlds, and so a Combinatorial theory of the conceivable.

One thing is clear, however. The introduction of distinct doxastically possible worlds that are not distinct worlds, and doxastically possible worlds that are impossible worlds, does require a Fictionalist or *Ersatz* treatment of these entities. A realistic theory of impossible worlds, in particular, is Realism gone mad. Impossible worlds are a conception, a conception which, like ideal gasses and frictionless planes, turns out to be useful in analysing actual phenomena. The conception is a thought-instrument.

But if we are not Realists about these 'worlds', why should we be Realists about possible worlds?

With Descartes the notions of the possible and the conceivable are very nearly run together. Provided only that what is conceived is 'clearly and distinctly' conceived, then, for Descartes, it is possible. And it seems that the subject himself is the infallible judge of clearness and distinctness. But, *contra* Descartes, it is of vital importance to separate the two notions, and to attain a precise conception of the conceivable. If, as I have argued in this section, they are both *Combinatorial* conceptions, then that would explain why it is so easy to confuse them.

6

Are there de re
incompatibilities and necessities?

I INTRODUCTORY REMARKS

In this chapter we examine a serious difficulty for Combinatorialism.

The Combinatorialist scheme depends on all combinations of universals being compossible. It should be possible for a single individual to instantiate any such combination, provided only that the universals so combined are *wholly* distinct, having no common constituents. For if we do not have this promiscuous compatibility, then we get logical incompatibility of a sort not envisaged by the theory.

If we consider what passes for properties and relations in our ordinary thinking, however, then we find that failures of compossibility abound. Consider properties first. These characteristically appear in *ranges,* so that they form classes of determinates falling under the one determinable. An individual can, at one time, instantiate only one member of this given range. The colour incompatibilities are a notorious instance of this phenomenon. Historically, they seem to have furnished one of the reasons Wittgenstein had for abandoning the metaphysics of the *Tractatus*.

Problems also arise in the case of relations. Restricting ourselves for the sake of simplicity to dyadic relations, problems are raised by symmetrical, by asymmetrical and by transitive relations. If a has symmetrical R to b, then it is entailed that b has R to a. If a has asymmetrical R to b, then it is excluded that b has R to a. If, finally, a has transitive R to b, and b has R to c, then these two states of affairs entail a third state of affairs: a's having R to c. But all this apparently contradicts the logical independence of states of affairs demanded by Combinatorialism.

The idea that these incompatibilities, or, in the case of transitivity, this necessity, are fundamental features of reality may be called an 'Aristotelian' ideal. Against this we are opposing the Leibnizian ideal where all simple properties are compossible. (For an illuminating discussion of the contrast, see Ruth Millikan [1984], especially pp. 268–9.) But unlike Leibniz we admit relations and allow the doxastic possibility that nothing is simple.

It must be admitted that the Aristotelian view does better justice to the surface of things. To adapt a justly famous phrase of Wilfrid Sellars's, it gives us the *manifest image* of properties and relations. Nor do I know how to disprove the view of many philosophers that this manifest image is a true image. All I can plead is that the Leibnizian view discovers a deeper order beneath the Aristotelian semi-chaos, and leads us to the agreeable intellectual simplicities of the Combinatorial theory.

II   INCOMPATIBLE PROPERTIES

I begin by considering the problem of incompatible properties. The previous chapter has provided us with certain resources. For instance, we have seen how the qualities that appear incompatible to perceivers could have a concealed element of negativity built into them. Given suitable positives and negatives, this could produce apparently incompatible properties.[1] I believe, however, that the most hopeful line of approach to the incompatibilities met with in practice lies in considering certain structural properties, in particular those linked with extensive quantities.

Consider, for instance, the properties of *being of mass of just five kilograms* and *being of mass of just one kilogram*. Obviously they are distinct (different) properties.[2] But they are not wholly distinct. Indeed, it is not obvious that the two properties contain any difference in their *constituents* at all. For to be of mass of just five kilograms is to be five wholly disjoint things of mass of just one kilogram: the very same universal five times instantiated.

Earlier, we said of complex universals that they are not merely embedded in states of affairs, but that they embed states of affairs.

---

1 Leibniz himself favoured a solution along these lines.
2 Bigelow and Pargetter (1988) argue that quantities should be construed as *relations*, not properties. The masses of individual objects, for instance, are to be 'constructed' from such relations as *being twice as massive as*. I criticize them and argue for the more natural property view in my 1988 article.

This seems helpful in understanding our present case. For something to be just five kilograms in mass is (among other things) for it to be the conjunction of five states of affairs involving five wholly distinct individuals each just one kilogram in mass, where the original something is the mereological sum of these five distinct individuals. Given this, it becomes clear why the very same thing cannot be both five and one kilogram in mass. To attempt to combine the two properties in the one thing would involve the thing's being identical with its proper part.

My suggestion is that this is a model for the logical incompatibilities of properties, or at least for their typical cases. Ranges of determinates falling under a determinable are extensive quantities. These are structural properties, involving parts lying outside parts, that is, involving conjunctions of states of affairs where the individuals involved in the states of affairs are wholly distinct from each other. The attempt to bestow two different determinates of such quantities on the one individual must fail. If the individual has the larger value of the quantity, then the only relevant individuals that have the smaller value are proper parts of the individual.

It would seem that the *quantities* which natural science deals so extensively in, and in particular the quantities recognized by physics, can, in general, be treated as structural properties of this sort. At any rate, such treatment seems a promising research programme. These quantities are among the best candidates we have for organized classes of universals. Their ranges are a fruitful source of incompatibilities.

But now to consider some doubts and difficulties about this suggestion.

First, a query may be raised about the status of the mereological principles used in this solution. To be just five kilograms in mass is to be made up of wholly distinct proper parts each of which is just one kilogram in mass, and to be just one kilogram in mass is to be a mere proper part of something that is just five kilograms in mass; *hence* a five-kilogram object cannot be just one kilogram in mass. But is this not a modal principle, and so one which, in my view, is to be analysed combinatorially rather than used to forbid certain combinations?

The question is a good one, and my answer to it is twofold. First, it would seem to be a real gain to base the obscurity of other modal principles on the clarity of principles concerning whole and part.

Second, I think it is reasonable to trace the necessity of these latter principles, the explanation why they hold in every possible world, to their *analyticity*. 'Analytic' here is to take its strongest sense. In this sense, a proposition is analytic if and only if it is true solely in virtue of the meanings of the terms in which it is stated. It seems plausible to say that the truth that a proper part of an entity is not identical with that entity is true solely by virtue of the meaning we attach to 'proper part'.

Second, it might seem that the solution would fail for *irreducibly intensive* quantities. The solution is tailor-made for extensive quantities, such as volume, duration and, I have assumed in the preceding discussion, mass. If an individual has an extensive quantity, then it has parts which lie outside each other, that is, which are numerically different from each other, and which go together to make up the individual and to give the individual the particular quantity that it has. As a result, a lesser quantity can only qualify a proper part of the individual. The solution cannot be directly applied to an intensive quantity such as density. But density is not irreducibly intensive. It can be resolved into, and so is supervenient on, volume and mass. As a result, incompatibilities of density can be resolved into incompatibilities of volume and mass.

Suppose, however, that there are *irreducibly* intensive quantities which exhibit incompatibility. Let Q be such a quantity. Suppose that an individual has degree Q_2 of quantity Q, which is greater than Q_1. It seems that this individual will not contain as a part an individual which has Q just to degree Q_1. As a result, we will not be able to explain the incompatibility of Q_2 and Q_1 in the way that we did for extensive quantities. As a matter of fact, there are grounds for thinking that, at a fundamental level, our example of mass is irreducibly intensive. For the truly fundamental particles are thought of as *point*-masses, yet different types of such particles have different masses.

It may be, however, that whatever quantities natural science sees fit to postulate, there is never any need to treat them as anything but superficially intensive. The problem with an *irreducibly* intensive quantity is that there would be no way of representing the 'parts' of a particular degree of that quantity as numerically different things, as one can where extension and duration are involved in the nature of the quantity. The underlying assumption here is that if *a* and *b* are numerically different, then they must be in different places, or, perhaps better, different place-times. Now difference of place-time seems to be sufficient (for individuals) to ensure non-identity. But the idea that sameness of place-time *ensures* identity of individuals is a more controversial notion, and one that has been quite frequently challenged in recent discussions. So why should we not say that *if* science sees fit to postulate apparently irreducible intensive quantities, then what is really being postulated is the simultaneous presence of many individuals at the same place? An individual at a certain place has a certain determinate of determinable quantity Q. No individual at that place and at that time has any greater value of Q. But to have this quantity is, essentially, to be made up of numerically different parts, but where the numerically different parts are individuals all to be found at that place and time.

There would appear to be no reason why, if scientifically required, the numerically different individuals should not be numerically different parts of an individual which was strictly continuous, just as for objects having ordinary extensive quantity-properties. If so, non-integral relations of proportion of different determinates of these determinable quantities could be provided for.

If all this is accepted, an apparently 'irreducibly intensive' quantity reduces to a structural property like volume, and incompatibilities of such quantities can be handled within the scheme already proposed.

Another way to deal with intensive quantities might be this. Consider a property such as electric charge. It appears to be intensive. Charge gives rise to attractions to and repulsions from other charged particles. These attractions and repulsions in turn give rise to motions or lack of motion. Motion and rest, however, can be cashed in terms of distances and times, which are extensive quantities. The charge itself could be treated as a mere *disposition* of the charged particle to attract and repel other particles according to certain formulae.

The disadvantage of this solution is that the disposition, if it is not to be a bare disposition, must be determined by categorical properties in the charged object which, together with the relevant laws of nature, determine the behaviour of charged particles. But it is hard to see what these further properties could be except quantities, quantities which, to avoid regress, would have to be extensive. This would again commit us to the charged objects having some sort of parts.

81

But third, there is the problem of incompatibilities among secondary qualities in the same range, in particular the colour-incompatibilities. The correct way to deal with them, I believe, is to say that they *are* structured properties like volume, duration and mass, but that their structure does not present itself to perception in the relatively perspicuous way that is the case with these primary qualities.

This solution, or something close to it, seems to be the one entertained by Wittgenstein in the *Tractatus*. He writes in 6.3751:

For example, the simultaneous presence of two colours in the visual field is impossible, in fact logically impossible, since it is ruled out by the logical structure of colour.

Let us think how this contradiction appears in physics: More or less as follows – a particle cannot have two velocities at the same time; that is to say, particles that are in different places at the same time cannot be identical.

The second paragraph appears to be proposing a solution in terms of structural properties. Suppose that at a certain instant, t, a moves with uniform velocity in a straight line for a second and covers a distance of *two* inches. At the same instant, b moves with uniform velocity in a straight line for a second and covers a distance of *one* inch. At $t + 1$ seconds a has the relational property of being two inches from where it was at t. However, at $t + 1$, b has the relational property of being one inch from where it was at t.

These relational properties, however, are structural properties. And they are such that a two-inch distance is made up of two numerically distinct one-inch distances. So to be two inches distant at a certain time from a certain point involves being numerically different from what is one inch distant from that point at that time. The two structural properties are distinct, but not wholly distinct, and the attempt to give the very same individual the two properties yields an impossible world. Thus, a must be different from (non-identical with) b. That, I take it, is the sort of reasoning Wittgenstein had in mind.

Whether these structural properties with which the secondary qualities are identified are taken to be primary properties of processes in the brain, or of external things, is immaterial here (although I strongly favour the latter). The great difficulty with either identification is phenomenological. The secondary qualities appear to be other than the primary qualities, having a nature of their own which is very much simpler than the primary-quality structures with which they would have to be identified.

I believe that these 'Leibniz law' difficulties can be overcome, at least to the extent of showing that the identification is not ruled out. We have already seen (Chapter 5, Section II) that an *and* neuron may register a complex stimulus, a structure perhaps, in a simple way. Various different inputs due to different features of a structure might be summed by the neuron. If, and only if, the sum is completed, the neuron reacts, but only in a simple, all-or-nothing, way. The structure would be registered as a simple.

The story can be continued by making reference to the Headless Woman illusion (Armstrong 1968). In this illusion, a failure to perceive a woman's head is translated by the mind into a false impression that the woman lacks a head. It seems to reflect a natural operator-shift in the human mind from lack of awareness to 'awareness' of a lack.

Suppose the identifications of secondary qualities with primary-quality structures are correct. We are certainly not perceptually aware that these qualities are identical with primary qualities. Phenomenologically, this lack of awareness translates into 'awareness' of a lack. The same point holds in the case of lack of awareness of the complexity (a positive factor) of the primary-quality structures. This translates again into 'awareness' of a lack of complexity.

It may still be objected, however, that the secondary qualities, especially colour, give an overwhelming impression of *quality*. Can it be that we are aware of nothing of the nature of these qualities except the sorts of objects they qualify and the sorts of ways we have of detecting them? This is the conclusion we would have to draw, it seems, if the suggested identification is correct.

But this objection overlooks the fact that we are aware of the secondary qualities as set in complex quality-spaces, spaces which psychologists and others are only now beginning to map in detail. These quality-spaces map the *resemblances* of ranges of qualities along various dimensions. Now resemblance, whether of individuals or qualities, is an internal relation, and, because internal, is logically supervenient on the intrinsic nature of the related terms. What is more, awareness of resemblance is naturally attributed to the nature of the resembling terms, *even where we are not directly aware of that nature*. As a result, I suggest, awareness of position in a quality-space naturally congeals into an impression of awareness of intrinsic nature. (For more discussion, see my 1987 article defending the Smart-Lewis-Armstrong account of the secondary qualities.)

As for our awareness of incompatibilities of the secondary qualities, this, I think, is rather neatly explained by the hypothesis that what we are really dealing with are incompatible (primary) quantities. Suppose, for instance, that a thing feels to have, and has, a certain weight. That weight is registering. If the weight had been greater, that greater weight would also have registered. The fact that it is not registering, together with the actual registering, is therefore being registered, even though the absence of the greater weight is not literally a causal factor. We have a *not* neuron or *not* neural assembly, as introduced in Section II of the preceding chapter. Hence, that a certain weight is being registered *but no greater weight,* makes the perceived weight incompatible with other possible weights for the individual. It is like the Headless Woman illusion, but here it operates to apprehend the world rightly.

If ranges of secondary qualities are ranges of quantities, then the same mechanism could be operating to produce awareness of incompatibilities of secondary qualities.

In this way, I suggest, the Combinatorialist can defend in more depth the view about the secondary qualities already adumbrated by Wittgenstein. We can then explain the incompatibility of these qualities within a Combinatorialist scheme.

III INCOMPATIBLE RELATIONS

Relations also raise problems. Consider symmetry first. If *a* has R to *b,* and if this entails that *b* has R to *a,* and vice-versa, then, *prima facie,* we have two distinct states of affairs. But then Combinatorialism would allow contraction. Either state of affairs might exist without the other. By hypothesis, however, this is not a possibility.

This seems not to create a serious problem. Suppose that *a* is a certain distance from *b.* Necessarily, *b* is at that distance from *a.* The obvious thing for a Combinatorialist to say is that these states of affairs are identical: two ways of symbolizing the same state of affairs.[3]

---

3 David Lewis has reminded me that this involves questioning the orthodoxy that associates *all* relations with *ordered* pairs. So be it. I do question it.

We turn now to asymmetry. If a is before b, then it is entailed that b is after a, and apparently excluded that b is before a. With respect to the first entailment, once again it seems correct to say that we have the one state of affairs described in two different ways. The inseparability of the 'two' states of affairs seems good evidence for this: Compare a causes b if and only if b is caused by a. Fairly obviously, this is just one state of affairs. The fact that if a is before b we do not say 'b is befored by a' instead of 'b is after a' would appear to be a relative linguistic accident.[4]

The exclusion of b being before a when a is before b is rather more troublesome, however. I think the best way to deal with it is to deny that this is really a necessary truth. Might not time be circular? I do not mean just that the doctrine of eternal return might be true, but that time might come round on itself. (Eternal return is the return of the qualitatively identical only.) If so, a and b would both be before and after each other. If the circularity or non-circularity of time is a contingent matter, then the proper independence of 'a is before b' and 'b is before a' is established.

Perhaps other cases of apparent necessary asymmetry can be dealt with similarly, at any rate where the relations are external.

The qualification that the relations be external is important. If a is larger than b then it seems logically excluded that b is larger than a. But this is a case of an internal relation. I shall be arguing in Chapter 8 that internal relations are all supervenient on properties (including relational properties) of the related terms. This means that such relations are not entities wholly distinct from their terms. And if so, the Combinatorial scheme does not have to treat these relations as freely available for recombination.

But what of transitivity? If a is before b, and b before c, then, is it not necessary that a is before c? Yet these relations are external. Different stratagems may be tried here. One I find appealing is to argue that a's being before c is in fact supervenient on the first two states of affairs. An analogy, or it may be more than analogy, can be drawn with causation.

We require first a notion of direct causation. In direct causation event a causes event b *without causal intermediary*. Let this be the fundamental relation of causality. Suppose then that a directly

---

4 Timothy Williamson has argued in detail that a relation and its converse are identical (1985).

causes *b* and *b* directly causes *c*. We would say that *a* causes *c*. But is this *direct* causation? I do not think it is. The plausibility of this contention emerges when we consider that, besides *b*'s causing *c*, *a* might also cause *c* without causal intermediary, so that the causing of *c* was a case of overdetermination. Given a relation of direct causation, we can give a recursive definition of indirect causation, and can see that *a*'s causing *c* *via* *b* is a case of indirect, not direct, causation. And then indirect causation is supervenient: *a* really does cause *c*, but ontologically there is nothing but *a* (directly) causing *b*, and *b* (directly) causing *c*.

But what if causal chains of this sort segment *ad infinitum?* For instance, *a* breaks down into *a'* succeeded by *a"*, with *a'* bringing about *a"*, these in turn breaking down so that direct causation is never reached. The answer is that even so, we can form the notion of *relatively direct* causation: *a"* causing b, for instance, is relatively direct by comparison with *a* causing b. Provided that in forming possible worlds the causal chain is always segmented into wholly distinct relative atoms, the causal relations that supervene on these atoms can be ignored. The atoms themselves can freely be recombined, with or without causal relations between them.

It may now be suggested that where *a* is before *b*, and *b* before *c*, that *a* is before *c* supervenes on the first two states in the same way that, I have just argued, holds in causal chains. In the temporal case also we can distinguish between direct and indirect temporal relations. This would be simply explained if, as I suspect, the temporal order *is* a causal order.

This discussion of relations has not been thorough. But I hope enough has been said to show that the thesis that *wholly distinct* relations are always compossible can be maintained with some degree of plausibility. A little more light may be cast by the discussion of causation in Section III of the next chapter.

7

Higher-order entities, negation and causation

I HIGHER-ORDER ENTITIES

In his article 'Tractarian Nominalism' (1981) Skyrms raises the question, 'In what sense is Tractarian Nominalism nominalism at all?' He then remarks, 'It is certainly not nominalism in the sense of Goodman ["A world of individuals"] or Quine ["On what there is"], since it finds quantification over properties and relations . . . just as acceptable as quantification over individuals, and cashes both in terms of facts' (p. 202).

Skyrms's *facts,* of course, are our *states of affairs.* Only the terminology is different. And since for Skyrms, as for us, different individuals may have the same property or be related by the same relation, and that in no mere Pickwickian sense, his properties and relations can fairly be described as universals. So why Tractarian *Nominalism?* Nominalists reject universals.

Skyrms goes on to answer his question thus:

Its properties and relations are all properties and relations *of* [first-order] individuals and its facts are all *first-order* facts: facts 'about' individuals. There are no higher-order facts. (p. 202)

By way of clarification, Skyrms makes an important qualification of this stand. He will admit 'higher-order' facts that are logically determined by first-order facts, but:

What the Tractarian Nominalist means to deny then is that there are any *autonomous* higher order propositions. *What he means to deny is that there are two distinct possible worlds which share all the same first order facts.* He will countenance only such higher order truths as are supervenient in this way on the first order facts.

Thus Tractarian Nominalism contrasts with the sort of free-swinging Tractarian Platonism which countenances all sorts of higher-order facts which are not so supervenient. (pp. 202–3)

To take the unimportant point first, I find Skyrms's terminological decision strange. Once he has admitted repeatable properties and relations, he has admitted universals, and so should reject the term 'Nominalism'. He may plead with some justice that he is not a swinger, and is only a little bit pregnant. But he is pregnant with universals none the less.

Passing to the substantive point, Skyrms's rejection of logically independent higher-order properties, relations and facts (states of affairs) must awaken a sympathetic response in any Empiricist breast. It is an ambitious and splendid piece of metaphysical simplification, a simplification which is one great source of the metaphysical attraction of the *Tractatus*. For, as Skyrms hints, to abandon this restriction is, apparently, to dismantle one's defences against the wildest metaphysical speculation.

Nevertheless, I believe we have to go up the ladder. If Platonism is defined as a doctrine of *transcendent* entities, then I do not think we have to embrace Platonism. We can remain Naturalists, staying within space-time. But we will have to enrich the structure of the space-time world. Indeed, we may be thought to have already done so when we allowed spatio-temporal particulars to instantiate universals (have repeatable properties and relations). To allow these instantiated properties and relations themselves to instantiate certain (carefully screened!) further universals – to have certain repeatable properties and to be related to each other – is perhaps no great extension.

I have already argued elsewhere (1983, Chapter 6) that an account of nomic necessity demands that we postulate relations between first-order properties, relations which are *not* supervenient on the first-order properties and their distribution over first-order individuals in space and time. Only so, I argued, could we escape the manifold implausibilities of the view that laws are mere regularities in the behaviour of things. To postulate such second-order relations between first-order properties is automatically to postulate second-order states of affairs: the holding of such relations between such properties.

As a matter of fact, a full development of the theory of laws of nature seems to demand higher-order *properties* as well. This springs from the necessity to accommodate *functional* laws (see Armstrong 1983, Chapter 7). Functional laws seem best analysed as *higher-order* laws. A typical functional law may be thought of as a determinable, with the indefinite multitude of laws obtained by feeding definite values into the antecedent conditions being the determinates of that determinable. The functional law cannot be thought of as nothing but the conjunction of all the determinate laws, however. That would resurrect the scepticism of a Humean view of laws at a higher level. It would leave unexplained a higher-level cosmic coincidence. It would also create difficulties for those determinates of the determinable laws whose antecedent conditions are nowhere and nowhen instantiated. What justification would there be for our confident extrapolations to such cases?

The solution, I think, is to recognize the functional law as a higher-order law governing the lower-order, determinate laws. But the functional law will have to link determinable properties, and these, it seems, will be properties of the determinate properties.

It may be thought that these higher-order properties and relations are a sort of 'optional extra' which the parsimonious will do well to avoid postulating. This attitude is at least weakened by the further reflection, to be developed in the next section, that higher-order entities are required even to account for facts of *negation* and *totality*. It is clear that ontological grounds, truth-makers, must be provided for negative truths: for instance, the fact that a certain individual does not instantiate a certain monadic universal. Consideration of this problem is bound up with a consideration of facts of totality, and it turns out that, to accommodate these facts, higher-order entities are required. Indeed, the very notion of a possible world cannot be defined in purely first-order terms.

It appears, however, that what are required for negation and totality are not higher-order properties and relations of first-order properties and relations (which I have just suggested are needed for analysing laws of nature) but rather higher-order *states of affairs* concerning *first-order* states of affairs.

But before going on to consider negation and totality we ought briefly to consider whether the introduction of higher-order entities does not sully the purity of our Combinatorial scheme by setting up logical linkages between distinct states of affairs.

I think that the offence to purity is not very great. First, *within* the higher-order states of affairs, Combinatorial principles can be applied with complete freedom. Suppose, for instance, that we analyse nomic connection in the way I favour, as a relation of necessitation or probabilification holding between wholly distinct universals. These higher-order states of affairs will be contingent: It will be possible to recombine universals promiscuously to yield merely possible nomic connections. As it happens, I have already argued, on independent grounds and with no conscious eye on Combinatorialism, that relations of nomic necessitation and/or of probabilification are irreflexive, non-transitive and non-symmetrical (1983, Chapter 10, Section 7). This is just as a Combinatorialist would desire. (We see here that the Combinatorialist must accept the thesis that the laws of nature vary in different possible worlds. This corresponds to the intuitions of many, if not all, philosophers.)

Second, the higher-order states of affairs required are *not* supervenient on first-order states of affairs. Given certain first-order states of affairs, it is never entailed that any higher-order states of affairs even *exist*. For instance, given the uniformity that all Fs are Gs, with F and G universals, it by no means follows that F-ness necessitates G-ness. It might be cosmic coincidence rather than law.

But third, I think it must be conceded that *if* there are higher-order states of affairs, then certain first-order states of affairs must exist. If universals could exist uninstantiated, then, as Michael Tooley has suggested, we could have F-ness necessitating G-ness without Fs or Gs (noted in Armstrong 1983, p. 165 *n.*). But if universals are but abstractions from states of affairs, as earlier argued, then, although real, they cannot exist without being instantiated in first-order states of affairs.

I think, however, that the relation of first-order states of affairs to their *constituents* provides us with a model, and a precedent, for the relation of higher-order states of affairs to lower-order states of affairs. We may say that the existence of a first-order state of affairs necessitates because it *presupposes* the existence of its constituents. In the same way, higher-order states of affairs necessitate because they presuppose certain lower-order states of affairs.

The latter necessitation may still seem mysterious, or 'magical' as David Lewis might put it. The best way to try to make it perspicuous is to begin with the simple case: second-order *properties*. Suppose that the determinate masses (*being one kilo, being a quarter ton*, etc.) are universals. Suppose that each of these universals falls under the universal of *being a mass*. (Such a falling under is not automatic. Remember that higher-order universals do not supervene.) We would have M(K) – where K = *being one kilo* – a second-order state of affairs. Suppose further that the state of affairs K's being *a* obtains. If *a* falls under K, and K falls under M, then there is a sense in which *a* falls under M. It would be wrong to say that *a* is a mass, but we can say that it has a mass, or is massy. This holds for *any* individual that is K. After all, K, being a universal, is everywhere the same. So it is excluded that there is an *x* which has K but is not massy. This seems perspicuous enough.

But now suppose that there is a (non-supervenient) relation holding between the universals F and G. This relation is such that something's being an F makes it to be the case that (ensures that, brings it about that, necessitates that) the same something is a G. F and G are everywhere the same. Given this relation between F and G, then, if *a* is F, then it is excluded that *a* is not G, and so for every other instance of F.

Again this seems perspicuous enough. If it is found difficult, then I think a large part of the trouble must be with the notions of *making it be the case that, ensuring that, bringing it about that, necessitating that.* But that these are troublesome to so many philosophers must, I think, be due to Humean scepticism about such notions. Hume's rejection of causality (for really it is a rejection) goes deep in our philosophical tradition. But in fact we appear to have direct experience of *making it to be the case that, ensuring that, bringing it about that, necessitating that,* at least in the particular case. I am thinking especially of our direct experience of causal action on our bodies, in the perception of pressure.

Two further remarks before leaving the topic. First, it may well be that the true and ultimate laws of the world are irreducibly probabilistic rather than necessitating. But I suggest that in such a case the relationship between the universals involved gives a certain (objective) *probability,* a probability less than 1, that the antecedent conditions should *necessitate* (bring about) the consequent.

Second, it is to be noticed that in the case of this relation of necessitation holding between universals there is a possibility that is not present in the case of properties of universals. Given a necessitating antecedent of a certain sort – a certain universal – there is the possibility of its operation's being blocked by the presence of a further factor. The situation is a familiar one. Forces of a certain sort are operating on a certain body. If these forces operate, and no others, then the body will behave in a certain way. But if in addi-

91

tion to these original forces there are other countervailing factors present, then the original effect may be wholly or partly cancelled. An F → G law, then, may be defeasible. F in the further presence of H may fail to produce G.

It may be said that in such a case the antecedent condition of the F → G law simply requires to be stated at greater length. It is F in the absence of H, and of any other factor that might interfere. But the difficulty for me in this formulation is that a Combinatorialist will not wish to recognize negative universals. *F and not-H* is not a universal.

I suggest, therefore, that we accept that an F → G law, a relationship between the two universals, does not necessitate that *each* F be a G, even where the law is non-probabilistic. Rather it is necessitated only that each F *which is not accompanied by interfering factors* is a G. Such interfering factors will always be found in some possible world. If they are not found in the actual world, then the F → G law may be called 'iron'. But if positive factors can *in fact* modify the operation of F with respect to G, then the law is merely 'oaken' (see Armstrong, 1983, Chapter 10, Section 4).

All this, I hope, is compatible with saying that such relations between universals only have logical consequences for first-order states of affairs because they presuppose the latter, in the same way that first-order states of affairs presuppose the existence of their constituents.

II NEGATION AND TOTALITY

Suppose that *a* is not F, with F a universal. We have already denied, on Combinatorial and other grounds, that 'not-F' names a universal. Equally, *a*'s not being F is not a state of affairs: Combinatorialism cannot admit negative states of affairs. So what is it in the world that makes it true that *a* is not F?

We have another problem. Let a certain class or aggregate (it does not seem to matter much which we say) be all the Fs. This fact about this class or aggregate is not analysable as an atomic state of affairs or conjunction of such states of affairs. We may call this the problem of totality.

It turns out best to tackle the problem of totality first. With that solved, progress can be made with the problem of negation.

The problem of totality is the same one Russell called the problem of *general facts*. Not everybody has accepted that there are general facts. Anybody who holds that the only facts (states of affairs in my terminology) that there are, are atomic facts and their conjunctions (Wittgenstein in the *Tractatus*, Skyrms in 'Tractarian Nominalism') is forced to deny them. But I think there is little doubt that Russell is right. Great philosopher that he is, he goes straight to the extreme case, the supreme general fact. In *The Philosophy of Logical Atomism* he writes:

I do not think one can doubt that there are general facts. It is perfectly clear, I think, that when you have enumerated all the atomic facts in the world, it is a further fact about the world that those are all the atomic facts there are about the world, and that is just as much an objective fact about the world as any of them are. It is clear, I think, that you must admit general facts as distinct from and over and above particular facts. (p. 93)

Later in the same paragraph, however, Russell says,

I do not profess to know what the right analysis of general facts is. It is an exceedingly difficult question.

Let us see if we can make an advance on Russell here.

We are inquiring into the nature of totality, or allness. What is it about all the Fs that makes them *all* the Fs? First, it cannot be a relation that this totality has to something outside itself. This is clear from the case Russell considers: the case of the totality of things. There is nothing for that totality to be related to. Is it then a *property* of the Fs? If by 'property' is meant *non-relational* property, then the difficulty is that *being all the Fs,* while a property in some sense, is a *non-repeatable* property. It is not a universal. One could try to introduce a totality property which all such properties (that is, *being all the Fs, being all the Gs*) have in common. But this totality property would be supervenient on these non-repeatable properties, and so not of great interest to us.

A more attractive scheme is to go back to the idea that *being all the Fs* is a relational property, but to argue that this relational property is supervenient on a *relation* that that totality has to something *within* the totality. The totality stands in a certain salient relation, which we may call the T relation, to *being an F*. Another totality, or perhaps this one, stands in the same T relation to *being a G*. A certain conjunction of atomic states of affairs stands in the T relation to *being a state of affairs*. T is interesting because it seems to be a universal. It is also external, or contingent, *not* supervening on any conjunction of first-order states of affairs. A class or aggregate of Xs that has T to *being an X* is thereby constituted *the totality of Xs*.

So the suggested form of states of affairs of totality is T (a class or aggregate of Xs, *being an X*). We might say that the class or aggregate 'totals' or 'exhausts' the Xs.

This analysis of facts of totality will now give us assistance in analysing negation. But before we leave facts of totality let us consider some problems involved in the notion of the totality of all states of affairs.

First, David Lewis has raised with me the question whether the fact of totality is in fact, as Russell claims, non-supervenient. (Of course, the language of supervenience antedates Russell's work. Only the language, however.) How, asks Lewis, could two worlds be exactly alike in all lower-order states of affairs, yet differ in this higher-order state of affairs?

The answer, of course, is that the two worlds could not differ. But I claim that this is so only because a totality state of affairs has already been written into the description of the case. Suppose we had a list of the states of affairs in the two worlds, but with no totality condition given. It would not be the case that every world that contained those states of affairs was the same world. You get that result only if you add that the worlds contain *just* those states of affairs, that is, those states of affairs *and nothing more*. The 'nothing more' must have a truth-maker. I claim that that truth-maker is a totality fact or state of affairs, having the form I have tried to describe.

A second worry is the paradox of totality. Take the alleged totality of states of affairs. A state of affairs holds of this conjunction: It stands in the totality relation to *being a state of affairs*. This higher-order state of affairs, however, is a state of affairs to add to the original 'totality'. When added, we have a new totality, and a new higher-order state of affairs that this is the new totality. That new higher-order state of affairs must be added in turn, and so *ad infinitum*.

I suggest, however, that we can afford to be casual about this infinite series. For after the first fact of totality these 'extra' states of affairs *are* all supervenient. As such, we do not have to take them with ontological seriousness. These are the original states of affairs, the fact that these do constitute the totality of states of affairs, and ontologically nothing more.

Facts of totality do bring up a third, more serious, problem, however. I have said that such states of affairs are not supervenient on any lower-order conjunctions of states of affairs. But is there not a degree of supervenience? For, it seems, there is necessarily some conjunction of states of affairs, finite or infinite, which is the totality of states of affairs. Totality must be reached at some point, even if there is no particular point at which it has to be reached. Contrast the situation here with higher-order states of affairs which are genuinely non-supervenient on lower-order states of affairs. Suppose, for instance, that one takes laws of nature to be relations of nomic necessitation or probabilification holding between universals. The second-order states of affairs fail to supervene on first-order regularities and statistical distributions. Furthermore, it is possible that they, the second-order relations, could be entirely absent despite the occurrence of the first-order distributions. (This would be an example of what Frank Jackson has called a Hume world, a cosmic-coincidence world.)

My answer to this difficulty is to distinguish between the fact of totality taken as a determinable and the same fact taken as a determinate. However large the world is, even if for *every* infinite number there exists in the world that infinity of individuals, the world constitutes a totality. But that, I suggest, is a trivial truth. This determinable fact of totality, the fact that there exists some totality of facts which constitutes the world, supervenes on the existence of the world. What does not supervene is the determinate fact. That a certain specific conjunction of states of affairs constitutes the totality of states of affairs does not supervene. And here an external T relation holds between this totality and *being a state of affairs*.

The same point holds for the totality of *a*'s properties, for example. There must be such a totality. That fact supervenes. But it is not supervenient that F, G . . . , and so forth, constitute the totality of *a*'s properties. There *is* 'a degree of supervenience', but all we need do is recognize it.

A fourth problem is constituted by the *terms* of T relations. There is no particular problem with the first terms. They will be aggregates (conjunctions) of states of affairs, properties, and so forth. But for the second terms we require such things as *being a state of affairs, being a non-relational property of a*, and so on. What is the status of such terms?

Here I must confess to uncertainty. *Being a state of affairs* could perhaps be taken to be a universal. Certainly it is a pure type, with no admixture of particularity. But I do not know whether or not to account it a universal. *Being a non-relational property of a* is not a universal. There are, however, properties in the world which answer to the corresponding description, and this is an objective fact about such properties, although supervenient on certain states of affairs (*a*'s being F and so on). So what I need to say, apparently, is that T, a universal, can have such supervenient properties as terms. Accordingly, I say it and hope that this does not involve some concealed difficulty.

Now we are in a position to consider negative truths. Let it be true that *a* is not F. What makes it true? (Russell agonizes about negative facts in *Logical Atomism,* pp. 67–72.)

The first thing which should encourage us is that negative facts supervene on facts of totality (as Russell noted). Given all the lower-order states of affairs, and the further fact that these *are* all the states of affairs, then all the negative facts are fixed. Given that *a* is G and is H and that this is the totality of *a*'s properties, then it is entailed that *a* is not F.

At the same time, that *a* is not F does not entail that *a* is G and H, so the truth-maker or ontological ground for '*a* is not F' is not very clear. I suspect that was what baffled Russell.

It is here that Combinatorialism, and in particular its rejection of alien properties, comes to the rescue. Let us make the unrealistic supposition that F, G and H are atomic and are the only properties there are. It is then a necessary truth that *a* is not F if *and only if a* has G as the totality of its properties, or *a* has H as the totality of its properties, or *a* has G and H as the totality of its properties. The truth is necessary because it is true in every (combinatorially formed) possible world. The *only if* is synthetic and could be established *a posteriori* only (if the reader will pretend that the latter phrase makes sense in so contracted a universe). But it is necessary. We have here another 'Kripkean' necessity.

Given now the necessity of the *if and only if,* which gives us *two-way* supervenience, it would seem reasonable to say that the two truths '*a* is not F' and '*a* has G as the totality of its properties, or *a* has H as the totality of its properties, or *a* has G and H as the totality of its properties' have the very same truth-makers. So we can substitute the second truth for the first. We already have an analysis of truths of totality. In our particular case, it is a matter of the T relation's holding between a certain class or aggregate of a's properties and *being a property of a*.

Our second, substituted, truth is a disjunction of totality propositions. Disjunctive truths, however, are easily dealt with. If it is true that a is P *or* a is Q, then the only truth-maker required is a's being P, or a's being Q, although if a is *both* P and Q then the truth has two truth-makers, each sufficient by itself. In the case we are considering, only one of the disjuncts will obtain. So that disjunct, a fact of totality about a's properties, will be the truth-maker for 'a is not F'.

III CAUSALITY

If we consider token–causation, this particular cause bringing about this particular effect, then it is natural to think of it as a relation holding between states of affairs. It is not just that an individual brings about the existence of an individual. Some individual or collection of individuals *being a certain way* brings it about that an individual or collection of individuals *is a certain way*. Event causes event or some state of a thing sustains a state of a thing. All this is plausibly analysed in terms of what we have called states of affairs (perhaps very complex ones). But if causation relates states of affairs, we appear to have a higher-order relation.

It is, of course, possible to argue that this causal relationship is supervenient on a certain sort of context, a context of other first-order states of affairs. This is the view held by those who hold a Humean or Regularity theory of causation, Skyrms among them. Suppose, to work with a schematic example, that a is F, that a has R to b, and that b is H. This is the cause. The effect is that b' is G, where b and b' are successive states of a particular that endures through time, and are themselves particulars ('time-slices'). Suppose that all other cases where a particular is F, and has R to a particular which is H, are succeeded by the next temporal stage of the second particular being G. Then perhaps the original token-sequence, indeed each token-sequence, is constituted a causal sequence, but superveniently only.

If some such view is correct, then, of course, from the standpoint of a Combinatorial view, causation presents no new problems. Without wishing to argue the matter here, however, I am convinced that this reductive account of causation is as hopeless as a Regularity account of laws of nature.

In my 1983 book on laws, I argued, incidentally to the main line of argument and also somewhat unwillingly, for a *Singularist* theory of causation. I could see no apodeictic argument that led from *this* causing *that* in an individual case to any further fact, in particular to the further fact that this state of affairs falls under some law. I was there influenced by a well-known lecture by Elizabeth Anscombe (1971) where, in effect, she calls Donald Davidson's bluff on just this point.

I still think that there is something right in the Singularist view. But all that is right is this: Our *concept* of causation is Singularist. The conceptually fundamental notion of causation is token causation. There is no conceptual or *a priori* argument that will lead us *apodeictically* from singular causation to law-governed causation. It is not 'contrary to reason', to use Hume's phrase, that this should cause that and yet no law be involved. Let the states of affairs, with their precise properties and relations, have been precisely identified in the particular case. It certainly creates a presumption that in other cases just that cause will bring about, or have a certain probability of bringing about, just that effect. But I see no *a priori* way to elevate the presumption to a necessary truth. Hence I see no way to argue apodeictically that *any* singular causal sequence or connection is law-governed.

Nevertheless, we do all think in practice that there is some very close connection between cause and law. Suppose that we think that a certain token sequence is a causal sequence. How do we try to test this supposition? One main way, if it is available, is to try to *repeat* the sequence. We move from the token to the type. If repetition proves possible, then we think we are on to something. This suggests that we think the same cause yields the same effect, which in turn suggests that we think a causal sequence is a law-governed sequence. To get to the details, that is, to try to establish the exact cause and the exact effect, we deliberately vary certain factors in our repetitions, while leaving others constant. Are we not probing for the *exact* law that governs sequences of this general sort? Such procedure makes no sense otherwise. And in practice this enables us to establish the laws, or approximations to laws, which govern cases of token causation.

What moral should we draw from this? Prompted by a suggestion from Adrian Heathcote, it now seems to me that we have good *a posteriori* evidence (an inference to the best explanation) for the identification of singular causal connection with the instantiation of laws of nature, or some subclass of the laws of nature such as laws of sequence, or perhaps laws of transfer of energy.

Although *a posteriori*, the identification will be like the identification of heat with motion of molecules. If true, the identification will be a necessary truth, holding in all possible worlds. The identification gives us the essence of causation.

If this is the correct amount of the matter, then causality gives the Combinatorialist no *new* problems. If laws are what I claim them to be, that is, necessitating or probabilifying relations between universals, then these higher-order states of affairs do rule out certain combinations of states of affairs at the first-order level. If something's being F necessitates that something's being G, then this state of affairs plus *a*'s being F *excludes a's being* G in worlds where the antecedent condition holds. But it has already been argued that the relation of higher-order states of affairs to lower-order states of affairs resembles the relation of first-order states of affairs to their constituents, in not allowing free recombination. The lower-order entities fail to entail the existence of anything higher. The higher is not supervenient. But the higher, if it exists, always involves something at the lower level.

I argued in my 1983 book (Chapter 6, Section 4) that a state of affairs such as N(F, G) is not merely a relation between universals but is itself a universal. If this is correct, then when the states of affairs of *a*'s being F and *a*'s being G instantiate the law N(F, G), it is *the law,* itself and entire, which is instantiated in the situation.

If this is so, then in being aware of singular causal sequence one is aware of a law, though normally unaware of the law *as* a law. And, against Hume, I think it is plausible to suggest that, in favourable cases, we have an *impression* of cause, a sense-perception, every bit as direct as a perception of colour or heat (none of these being free from the possibility of misperception). The impression I am thinking of is the perception of pressure on our body.

What happens if the law involved is probabilistic only, as may be the case for the fundamental laws of our world? In that case I suggest that causation is still involved, but only where the consequent state of affairs actually occurs. As already mentioned in the previous section, I take a probabilistic law to be a relation between universals which gives a certain objective probability that an instance of the antecedent state of affairs will nomically necessitate (N) the consequent state of affairs. Perhaps causing is the relation N, or perhaps causing should be restricted to some subclass of the class of laws.

We have already spoken of *indirect* causation (Chapter 6, Section III). If C_1 causes C_2 and C_2 causes C_3, then C_1 causes C_3. But this latter is indirect causation, supervening on the chain of direct (or relatively direct) causes. In my 1983 book I called attention to the same phenomenon in the laws of nature (Chapter 10, Section 3). If $N(F, G)$ and $N(G, H)$, then we can *apparently* conclude that $N(F, H)$. In fact, however, although it seems fair to say that it is a law that Fs are Hs, I denied that it can be concluded that $N(F, H)$. All we have is a *derived* law. It could be symbolized as $N*(F, H)$. I did not use the terminology of supervenience, but it would have been appropriate. I could have also spoken of *indirect* nomic necessitation. If the argument of this section has been correct, indirect nomic necessitation and indirect causation are the same thing, or nearly the same thing.

IV APPLYING THE THEORY

The major difficulties for our theory have now been discussed. The difficulties are real, but not, I think, insurmountable. In the next chapter we can begin to reap some rewards. But before going on, it will be useful to pause and consider how the theory deals with claims that such-and-such is a genuine possibility.

What a statement states is a possibility if and only if there exists a possible world in which that statement is true. For us this means that there must be atomic or molecular states of affairs in some possible world which make the statement true, where possible worlds are combinations or recombinations of the actual entities in the world. Let us take as our example a case used by David Lewis (1986a), that of a talking donkey. Is this a possibility?

We begin by observing that a theory like Lewis's, and indeed any non-Naturalist theory of possibility, faces a serious epistemic difficulty. What reason has Lewis to think that he has any way of casting light on the question whether, in worlds other than this, there are talking donkeys? He has his modal intuitions, of course, and in particular he has distilled these intuitions into a principle of recombination. That principle at least suggests that a combination of donkeyhood and speech should be a possible one. But his organized modal intuitions are just thoughts within a this-worldly head. Why should he think that they give him any rational guidance about the structure of other worlds?

Surely Lewis can have no deductive reasons for believing there are talking donkeys in other worlds, even if we weaken the force of 'deductive' to include logical probabilities. Surely he can have no inductive reasons to believe in the existence of such donkeys, even where 'inductive' is expanded to cover all scientifically respectable general modes of reasoning. So what modes of reasoning are available to Lewis, and what reason is there to think that these modes are reasonable?

Not that Lewis is in any worse position than any other upholder of a non-Naturalist theory of possibility. How does Adams, for instance, make any rational decision on the question whether the proposition that there are talking donkeys is or is not included in some maximal sets of consistent propositions?

By contrast, the Combinatorialist faces a far less daunting, even if still-difficult, task. What makes a thing a donkey? Almost certainly, there is no universal of donkeyhood. What we now know of donkeys and the conditions of their existence renders this virtually certain. What we will have instead is a great family of structural universals, where the borderlines between members and non-members of the family is semantically undecided. Instantiating any member of this family will make a thing a donkey. There may be a further complication. Perhaps our concept of a donkey is such that certain lacks or absences of universals are required to make us count a thing a donkey. (Perhaps, although it does not seem very likely, we are semantically programmed to refuse the term 'donkey' to a talking being.)

What has just been said about donkeys would appear to hold for talking beings. Fundamentally it is a matter of a disjunctive range of structural universals, where instantiation of a disjunct makes a thing a talking being.

The task of the Combinatorialist is then relatively straightforward. All that is required for the possibility of a talking donkey is that the structural universals from the two ranges be such that at least one universal in the donkey range combines with some universal in the talking range to qualify the same individual in a possible world. Given the promiscuous nature of combination, this condition will fail only in special circumstances. It would fail, for instance, if a donkey falls within a certain range of shapes and sizes while a talking being falls within a non-overlapping range of shapes and sizes. This would destroy the non-overlapping nature of the relative atoms demanded in any recombination, because objects with two different sizes are always two different objects.

So it would appear that there is a strong case for thinking that a talking donkey is possible. But the important point is that the matter can be investigated and with luck decided in this world. There can be scientific investigation of the nature of donkeys and of talking. There can be investigation of the semantics of 'donkey' and 'talking'. Given this, the range of universals with which we are dealing can be established (or at least reasonably hypothesized), and any incompatibilities that these universals involve brought to light. These incompatibilities are determined simply on the grounds of the identity (including partial identity) or non-identity of the universals in question.

A Naturalist Combinatorialism, then, makes possibility epistemically accessible. The only Naturalist alternative for a theory of possibility seems to be that modality is an irreducible feature of this world – a theory of *de re* compatibilities and incompatibilities. It is worth remarking that the epistemology of this view is very obscure. How can one begin to decide, for instance, whether causal connection is a necessary or a contingent connection, given this view? Do *de re* necessities affect our minds differently from mere contingencies?

8

Supervenience

I THE NOTION OF SUPERVENIENCE

In the preceding four chapters the theory may be said to have been on the defensive. I have been trying to show that the theory can meet, or has reasonable prospects of meeting, certain difficulties. At this point, however, we can relax and draw certain more or less interesting consequences from the theory.

We have a theory of possible worlds intended to be compatible with Naturalism. We can go on to use the possible worlds to define the notion of supervenience, and then use the latter notion to draw metaphysical conclusions of great importance.

I propose to work with the following simple definition of supervenience: If there exist possible worlds which contain an entity or entities R, and if in each such world there exists an entity or entities S, then and only then S supervenes on R. For instance, if there exist worlds in which two or more individuals have the property F, then, in each world containing such states of affairs, these same individuals stand in the relation of resemblance (at least in some degree). These resemblances are therefore supervenient on the individuals in question having property F.

This definition allows there to be cases where not only is S supervenient on R, but R is at the same time supervenient on S. This does not hold in the case just considered. Consider the individuals which are all F, and which therefore all resemble one another. There are worlds in which just these individuals resemble one another, and to just the same degree, but in which some or all of these individuals lack F. There are other cases, however, in which the supervenience runs in both directions. For instance, all worlds that contain the individuals *a, b* and *c* contain an infinity of classes: There are first-order classes involving just one, two or all of these individuals, but also the higher-order classes formed from these classes. So the classes supervene on the individuals. But equally all worlds that contain these classes contain these individuals. So the individuals supervene on the classes.

This may seem somewhat unwelcome. It certainly goes against the suggestion implicit in the word 'supervenient' which creates the expectation of an asymmetrical relation. But it is in fact desirable at least to begin by allowing symmetrical superveniences. There may be a tighter definition of the notion, in terms of which the notion that I propose to work with is a necessary, but not sufficient, condition for supervenience. But a search for such a definition would be distracting rather than helpful at the present time.

Suppose that we have, or think we have, a supervenience relation. What metaphysical conclusions should we draw from it? If we are Combinatorialists, then I think the *general* conclusion to be drawn is pretty clear. Where there is supervenience, there the entities involved are not wholly distinct. For suppose that the entities involved were wholly distinct. Would not a Combinatorialist wish to decombine them and form worlds in which one of the sides of the supervenience existed without the other, *counting such worlds as possibilities?* And then supervenience, as we have defined it, would fail.

I think it is interesting to notice that many of those in contemporary metaphysics who work with the notion of supervenience seem tacitly to accept the inference 'if supervenient, then not wholly distinct'. (Skyrms for instance. Note the relaxed way that he allows higher-order propositions provided that they are supervenient, because they are not 'autonomous'. See Chapter 7, Section I, of this volume.) A supervenience thesis is often thought of as a *reductionist* thesis, or perhaps as a superior substitute for reduction. It is superior because it promises to cut down on entities without necessarily demanding that statements about the supervenient entities be *translated* into statements about the entities on which the supervenient supervenes. Perhaps it might be said to be ontologically reductionist, without being semantically reductionist.

It is to be noted, of course, that theses of supervenience are simply *theses*. Some of these theses are very controversial and serve more to focus an issue than to decide it. The Humean thesis about both cause and natural law is an important example. According to this now venerable Empiricist thesis, all causal and nomic states of affairs are supervenient on states of affairs which do not involve cause and law – roughly, matters of fact about particular times and

104

places. This is a supervenience thesis which I reject.[1] Nevertheless, as we shall see in this chapter, some theses of supervenience seem to be extremely plausible and suggest promising ontological simplifications. Internal relations are prominent candidates for supervenient entities, and I begin with a discussion of them.

II INTERNAL RELATIONS

As I shall use the term, objects having certain properties are *internally* related by relation R if and only if, in each possible world which contains these objects, and where they have these properties, the objects are related by the relation R. 'Objects' here should not exclude the singular case. In every world in which entity E exists, and regardless of what properties E has, E is identical with itself. So the relation of identity is an internal one. Note also that 'properties' in the preceding definition should be taken to include relational properties. If two objects both stand in relation R to an F, then an internal relation of resemblance holds between them. Of course, the relational properties appealed to as the ground of supervenience must not involve relational properties based on the very relation said to be internal.

If *a*'s having R to *b* is supervenient on *a*'s being P and *b*'s being Q, then we do not have combinatorial freedom. This means that we are not dealing with wholly distinct states of affairs. But since *a*'s being P and *b*'s being Q may well be states of affairs in good metaphysical standing, then it seems that we should say that in such a case *a*'s having R to *b* is not a state of affairs additional to the first two states of affairs.

Does this mean that internal relations are not really relations, that our 'R' is a dyadic predicate to which no genuine relation corre-

1 To reject such supervenience theses is not automatically to reject Naturalism, although Nominalists may be inclined to think it is. Universals, I think, are not supervenient on particulars, at any rate thin particulars, as for instance those who think of universals as mere classes of particulars must hold. But that is compatible with holding that all universals are spatio-temporal in the sense of being constituents of those states of affairs whose conjunction is space-time. The same may be said about relations between universals, and about causal relations. My idea is that instead of deserting spatio-temporal naturalism, we should rather enrich or soup up the ontological structure of space-time. The resultant world-view is still ontologically parsimonious. It is just that it does not try to do justice to the phenomena using only the exiguous equipment with which too many Empiricists have misguidedly, if heroically, tried to do the job.

sponds? There seems to be something in this, but at the same time we have to be careful what we say. Consider the internal relation of *having the same shape as*. If a has S_1 and b has S_1, then a and b stand in this relation. If c has S_2 and d has S_2, then c and d stand in the very same relation. But have not the pair $\{a,b\}$ and the pair $\{c,d\}$ *something in common?* Is there not here a *one* that might run through many pairs of things with the same shape? It is a somewhat abstract one, but it might even be causally important. For instance, possession of just this internal relation might be necessary and sufficient for pairs of things to elicit positive reaction from a sorting machine.

It seems that we might want to admit such a thing as *pairs having the same shape* as a universal, at any rate provided it turned out to play a causal role in the world. But I think it is right to deny that 'having the same shape as' is a genuine *relation*. What we have rather is a structural property of such objects as $[a + b]$ and $[c + d]$, a structural property of the minimal sort that does not involve any relation between a and b (or c and d): a *non-relational* structural property.

We pass on now to consider the question of what relations are internal. Hume, in a famous section of the *Treatise* (Book I, Part I, Section 5), tells us that all relations may be brought under just seven heads. The heads are resemblance, identity, relations of time and place, proportion in quantity or number, degree in any quality, contrariety and causation. Resemblance, proportion in quantity or number, degree in any quality, and contrariety he calls relations of ideas. These are what the moderns call internal relations.

It is generally granted, and seems fairly clear in itself, that resemblance is an internal relation. It has already been noticed that the supervenience relation goes one way but not the other. If a and b have certain determinate common properties, then a resemblance-relation supervenes. Yet it seems that, in general, there will be worlds in which a and b have just that degree of resemblance, but in which they have it in virtue of quite other determinate common properties. This suggests quite strongly that resemblance is to be analysed in terms of the natures of the resembling things, rather than the natures of the things being determined by their resemblances.

This point does not lead us directly from resemblances to common properties, that is to universals, although I think that is a plausible inference. For it is possible to block the inference by holding that resemblance supervenes not on *common* properties but the *particularized* natures of things, properties and relations which are particulars rather than universals, as in the philosophy of G. F. Stout and others. (Talk of different individuals having the 'same' properties is then analysed in terms of these particular properties' forming an equivalence class of exactly resembling properties.) But at least the internality of resemblance shows that the ontological weight must fall on the *natures* of resembling individuals, whether these natures be universals or particularized properties.

Numerical relations are fairly clearly internal. That the number of men in this group is greater than the number of men in that group supervenes on the nature of the two groups: their internal make-up. Incidentally, this points to the weakness of the Russell–Whitehead definition of number as a class of classes similar to (in one-to-one correspondence with) a given class. This similarity is supervenient, rather, on the nature of each of the classes. And what is the vital feature of that nature? It is the number of members each class has.

Relations of quantity provide interesting cases. I think it is natural to do as Hume in effect does, and treat them as internal relations, supervenient on the quantities so related. But it may be, and has been, argued that spatial size, for instance, is constituted by the size-relationships which hold between things which are compared in size, and that these relationships are external. This view may be put forward in an Operationalist or, more plausibly, a Realist version.

In the Operationalist version one relies on conditionals, for the most part counterfactuals, about what happens if one object is, for example, superimposed on another. These conditionals require a truth-maker, an ontological ground, something about the objects which are to be superimposed, that determines (presumably nomically determines) the hypothetical result of these operations. It cannot be the size of the object. But what else can it be?

A Realist relational view of the sort put forward by Bigelow and Pargetter (1988), where the relations are not cashed out in terms of hypothetical superpositions, and so forth, is more plausible. But surely there must be *something* about size-related things that gives them the size-relations they happen to have. It is difficult to find any candidate for this something except size-*properties*, but then the relations become internal. (For more detailed discussion see Armstrong [1988], criticizing Bigelow and Pargetter.)

Degree of quality will, in general at least, be an internal relation. That one object is hotter than another supervenes on the temperatures of the two objects.

Of contrariety Hume remarks that, strictly speaking, no ideas are contrary in themselves except existence and non-existence. But, we may add, there are no non-existent things, and so non-existence cannot have even an internal relation to existence. There are such things as logical relations of contrariety between propositions. But if states of affairs are to have the limited number of forms which have been attributed to them in this essay, then the actual contemplating of or assenting to contrary propositions, in one or more minds, must be a matter of states of affairs whose structure, however complex, is very different from the instantiation of a relation of contrariety.

We come now to external relations, called 'relations of matters of fact' by Hume. He says that they can all be subsumed under the heads of identity, spatio-temporal relation and causation.

By 'identity' Hume does not mean the identity of any entity with itself. That, we have already argued, is an internal relation, and Hume would surely agree. It may be added that *difference* is also an internal relation. Hume says that he does not include it in his list because 'it is rather the negation of a relation than anything positive in itself'. But while this would, in my view, exclude it if it were an external (i.e. genuine) relation, I see no reason to exclude it from the internal relations. For, as I have been arguing, the supervenient is not an addition to what it supervenes on.

Hume's identity is rather identity through time. What he in effect claims, and what other philosophers have claimed (but still others have denied), is that the identity of individuals through time is not genuine. What we call a thing at one time, and 'the very same thing' at a different time, are not genuinely identical. They are wholly distinct temporal parts. 'Identity through time' is the relation which welds these temporal parts into a whole (what John Perry calls 'the unity relation'; see his 1975, p. 12). For Hume, this relation is complex, and analysable. It is analysable in terms of *resemblance, spatio-temporal continuity* and *causation*.

But if analysable in this way, then 'identity through time' is not, as Hume is well aware, really a further category over and above the other six. Resemblance has already been considered, and declared internal. Spatio-temporal continuity is a subspecies of spatio-temporal relation. For Hume, then, the external relations are covered by the categories of spatio-temporal relation and causal relation.

I sympathize with Hume's approach to the problem of identity through time. I accept the notion of temporal parts. And for solving the unity problem, it seems to me that Hume is pointing in the right direction, especially with the introduction of causation. A continuing thing is some sort of causal process, a causal line as Russell put it (1948, pp. 333–4, 476–7, 507–9).

Acceptance of temporal parts seems to be the natural position for a Combinatorialist to take. For the times through which an enduring thing endures are surely divisible into wholly distinct times. And if so, it will at least be profoundly natural to divide the thing that exists at the successive times, as well as the times themselves, into temporal parts. But in any case, if temporal parts are denied, there will be a problem that Lewis calls the problem of accidental intrinsics, which I spoke of in Chapter 2, Section III. How can the *very* same thing possess a certain property at T_1 but lack that property at T_2? At the very least, some different conception of properties would be called for (e.g. a time-indexing of properties, or taking properties to be merely *related* to individuals) than that deployed in this work.

Suppose, however, that Hume is wrong, that individuals do not have temporal parts, but that a Combinatorial theory can still be developed. Identity through time will then just be identity, and so an internal relation.

So Hume has reduced the candidates for external relations to the categories of spatio-temporal and causal relations. These do appear to be external. If two things are at a distance from each other, for instance, then there would appear to be possible worlds in which the things exist, but are not at that distance or perhaps any other. Again, if one event causes another, there seem to be possible worlds in which the events exist, but causal connection is lacking.

The question then arises: Can the categories be reduced still further?

For Hume, of course, they can. For him, the ontological component of causation is nothing but regular succession. Causation is analysed in terms of temporal relation and resemblance. If this is correct, then the only external relations are the spatio-temporal relations, which would be a notable simplification.

I myself, for reasons set out in my 1983 book (Chapter 6, Section 5), do not accept Hume's reduction. Indeed, it seems to me to be a more hopeful course to attempt a reduction of at least some spatio-temporal relations to cases of (singular) causation. (The reduction would be an *a posteriori* but necessary identification.) The most plausible candidate for such a reduction is that feature of time which is not duplicated in space: the asymmetrical order of time. But I would not wish to rule out the (epistemic) possibility of further reductions.

In Section III of the preceding chapter, I further suggested that singular causal relations may plausibly be identified with the instantiation of laws, or, perhaps, with some particular subspecies of law, laws of transfer of energy perhaps. Again the identification would be *a posteriori* but necessary. These laws, as I conceive them, are *not* supervenient on regularities or statistical distributions at the level of first-order states of affairs. Instead, they involve higher-order relations between universals, relations that are external. So for me the external relations are restricted to spatio-temporal relations, nomic relations and, we must not forget, the 'totality' relations discussed in Section II of Chapter 7.

Some philosophers, while accepting that laws are relations between universals, hold that these relations are necessary (recently: Swoyer 1982; Shoemaker 1984, Chapter 10). This would make nomic relations into internal relations. But from the point of view of Combinatorialism this would trivialize the nomic relation. Internal relations are not really relations: ontologically, they are not anything over and above the terms and the natures of the terms from which the relation flows. Can this be all there is to nomic connection? It seems rather that a believer in the necessity of nomic connection between universals must accept 'necessary connection between distinct existences' in a stronger sense than a Combinatorialist can.

The same defence, be it noted, can be given (by a Combinatorialist) of the externality of spatio-temporal and causal relations.

From the point of view of the theses of this essay, however, much of the preceding is relatively negotiable detail. The important distinction from our point of view has been the original distinction between internal and external relations, followed by the claim, backed by a Combinatorial account of possible worlds, that internal relations are not something over and above the possession by the related things of certain properties. On any view, internal relations are ubiquitous. It is a great metaphysical simplification to reduce the genuine relations to the relatively sparse class of external relations. It is the latter relations only which yield Combinatorial material for 'different possible worlds'.

External relations may usefully be classified as *direct* or *indirect* external relations, although the distinction may be relative only. If *a* stands in the avuncular relation to *b,* then this is an external relation. There are possible worlds in which *a* and *b* both exist, but are not so related. But the relation is indirect. For it to obtain there must exist a third person who stands in the sibling relation to *a* and the parental relation to *b.* Given a state of affairs of the sort described in the preceding sentence, then the avuncular relation between *a* and *b supervenes.* So the relation is indirect, relative to the relations on which it supervenes. The sibling relation is also indirect relative to further relations to parents. Whether the world contains relations that are *absolutely* direct appears to be an empirical question.

We have already met with indirect external relations in discussing causal and nomic chains. If a state of affairs C_1 causes C_2 which in turn causes C_3, then C_1 can be said to cause C_3. If it is a law that whatever is F is also G: $N(F, G)$, and also a law that $N(G, H)$, then it can be said that it is a law that whatever is F is also H. But the causation of C_3 by C_1, and the $F \rightarrow H$ law, are indirect relative to the base indicated, and supervene on that base. It is particularly easy to overlook the indirect and supervenient nature of relations that obtain in a causal or nomic chain. No doubt this is because of the type-identity of the base relations.

III   FURTHER SUPERVENIENCES

In this section I deal briefly with a number of additional types of supervenience, of varying degrees of importance.

1. Conjunctive states of affairs. If wholly distinct states of affairs both obtain, say *a*'s being F and *b*'s being G, then, automatically and superveniently, in every possible world, the molecular state of affairs that is their conjunction obtains. The situation is symmetrical, however. If the molecular state of affairs exists, then in every case the atomic (or relatively atomic) states of affairs exist.

The moral to be drawn is that the molecular state of affairs and its conjuncts are not in any way distinct. This seems trivial enough in the example described. It would seem less trivial in a context where, for example, we were able to respond cognitively to just that molecular state of affairs, but were unable to dissect it into its atomic constituents, or even, perhaps, detect that it was complex.

2. Parts and wholes. The relation between molecular states of affairs and their constituent states of affairs appears to be a particular case of the relation of a whole to its parts. Wholes are supervenient on their parts, at any rate if we take wholes in the unambitious way proposed by the mereological calculus. We do not have to decide here whether any plurality of entities at all may be summed to make a whole. But if they do sum to a whole, then they sum to that whole (and to no other) in every possible world in which the parts exist. Equally, however, the parts are supervenient on the whole: given the whole, the parts will always be there.

The moral is clear: The mereological relations, what D. C. Williams calls the *partitive* relations (1966, Chapter 13), are internal, and so nothing additional to their *relata*.

3. Sets. We come now to a much more puzzling supervenience. Given a number of objects that are not sets, we can form first-order sets from them, and then proceed *ad infinitum* to form higher-order sets. All these sets are supervenient on the original objects: there is no possible world that contains the objects and lacks the sets. Equally, of course, the objects are supervenient on the sets, because sets take their identity from the members that they have.

To the Combinatorialist, at least, this will suggest that what we have here is an identity: the very same thing described in different ways. At any rate, we must reject the suggestion that sets are 'abstract' entities, metaphysically orthogonal to their ultimate members. If this were accepted, the Combinatorialist will argue, then sets and their members could be separated in some possible world. But this consequence is absurd.

But what are sets, then? We are faced with the fact that set theory is unassailably useful, and presumably useful because true. Yet how can objects be linked with the complex set-structure in which they are embedded? My suggestion is that the word 'embedded' may give us a clue. There are things in which, given the ontology that

112

has been defended in this essay, individuals are embedded. These are states of affairs. Perhaps sets are states of affairs?

The suggestion cannot be worked out further at this moment. But we will return to sets in the next chapter.

4. Conjunctive universals. If *a* instantiates both F and G, where F and G are wholly distinct universals, then *a* instantiates the conjunctive universal *F&G*. The existence of the conjunctive universal supervenes on these states of affairs. But, of course, there may be other states of affairs on which the very same universal supervenes. As a result, the supervenience relation is not symmetrical. No particular state of affairs supervenes on the existence of the conjunctive universal.

Why recognize conjunctive universals? Why not simply recognize the states of affairs on which they supervene? I offer three reasons. First, the conjunction is one that can run through many individuals at any place and time. Second, we have noted that it is at least doxastically possible that *every* universal is conjunctive (Chapter 5, Section I). Third, the conjunction of universals may figure as antecedent or consequent in a law of nature, where what the conjunction necessitates or probabilifies is no mere sum of what the individual conjuncts do by themselves.

There are those who would set weaker conditions for conjunctive universals. They would demand merely that F and G be co-instantiated in some possible world. But given our Actualist-Naturalism we do better to think of this demand as giving us only a *possible* universal. And there is no reason to say that all possible universals are universals, any more than there is reason to say that all possible particulars are particulars.

5. Structural universals. The supervenience of structural universals follows the same pattern as conjunctive universals. Indeed, the latter may be thought of as the simplest cases of structural universals. If *a* is F and *b* is G, with *a* wholly distinct from *b,* and if *a* has R to *b,* then it is a supervenient fact that the individual [*a* + *b*] instantiates the structural property *made up just of an F-part having R to a wholly distinct G-part.* As with conjunctive universals, structural universals are ones that can run through many; it is doxastically possible that all universals are structural ('structures all the way down'); and structural universals may be irreducible terms of laws of nature.

6. Relational properties. If *a* has R to *b,* and *b* is an F, then there supervenes on these states of affairs that *a* has the relational property of *having R to an F*. If conjunctive and structural universals are admitted, then this relational property should also be admitted as a universal. Such a property might figure as an irreducible term in a law of nature. It is impossible, however, for every universal to be a relational property. Individuals must have some non-relational properties.

Relational properties are a sort of mirror image of internal relations. They might be called 'external properties'. The parallel becomes most clear if we consider correlative pairs of relational properties such as *being a husband* and *being a wife*. If a man and a woman stand in the (more or less) external relation of marriage, then, superveniently, the man has the relational property of *being a husband* and the woman the relational property of *being a wife*.

If we consider simply *a*'s having R to *b*, then supervenient on this state of affairs is a relational property in an extended sense: *having R to b*. Such a property is like a universal in being 'predicable of many', because other individuals can have R to *b*. But it does not have the complete lack of restriction that a genuine universal has. Since these properties are supervenient, however, to recognize them involves no ontological cost beyond our original outlay: states of affairs involving individuals, properties and relations.

7. Disjunctive properties. Suppose that F and G are universals, that *a* is F but not G, while *b* is G but not F. Can we say that *a* and *b* both have the disjunctive property *F or G?* I used to reject this conclusion. But the simple reflection that this property is supervenient on the existence of the universals F and G seems to make disjunctive properties admissible because, ontologically, they are no addition to the universe.

What is true about disjunctive properties is that they are not universals, and so properties only in a second-rate sense. They are not *ones* that run through many. (Peter Forrest has suggested that they could be called 'multiversals'.) They will play no part in the construction of possible worlds. (Contrast conjunctive and structural properties which could serve at least as *relative* atoms.)

But it is very useful to talk about these second-rate properties, especially in situations where it is not known whether they are mere disjunctions or genuine universals (see Chapter 5, Section II, where we considered the situation where either of two properties triggers the same firing of a certain neuron). Wittgenstein's reflections on family resemblances have shown us how valuable it can be to have available a disjunctive conception for dealing with the sorts, kinds and properties of ordinary language. We shall see in the next chapter that disjunctive properties are required in the elucidation of the concept of *number*. So I now admit such properties, and excuse them for not carving up the beast of reality along its true joints.

8. Negative properties. But if we admit disjunctive properties, we can hardly disbar negative properties. For they too are supervenient, although their supervenience is a much more complex affair than the disjunctive case, a greater complexity only to be expected when it is remembered how much philosophical puzzlement negation has engendered. Suppose that *a* is not F, with F a universal. Then, as argued in Section II of the preceding chapter, there is a state of affairs, in general a conjunctive state of affairs, which is the possession by *a* of all its properties (pleonastically, positive properties). There is a higher-order state of affairs, a fact of totality, involving the T relation between the collectivity of *a*'s properties and *being a property of a,* that this conjunction exhausts *a*'s properties. The negative properties of *a* are all supervenient on these two states of affairs.

Given this supervenience, and given the usefulness of admitting negativity as a possible element in our *ordinary* conception of properties, it seems that negative properties can be admitted in the same spirit as disjunctive properties.

9. Supervenient states of affairs. To admit disjunctive and negative properties raises the question whether we should not admit states of affairs involving the 'instantiation' of disjunctive and negative properties. Equally, why should we not admit disjunctions of 'proper' states of affairs, together with negations of merely possible but proper states of affairs, as themselves being states of affairs?

I think the answer is once again that we can do this if we please, and do it without ontological cost, because these second-rate states of affairs are supervenient on the metaphysically fundamental states of affairs. And the manoeuvre turns out to be useful, particularly in connection with the idea, still to be expounded, that sets are states of affairs.

IV HUME'S DISTINCT-EXISTENCES PRINCIPLE

An interesting feature of our Combinatorial scheme is that a (non-psychological) version of Hume's Distinct-Existences Principle drops out of it. The principle itself is somewhat controversial. Some philosophers are inclined to accept it, others to reject it. So the derivation of the Principle from Combinatorialism does not here supply us with an independent argument confirming Combinatorialism. Some may even think that we can argue from the falsity of the principle back to the falsity of Combinatorialism. In effect, those who hold that there are primitive, unanalysable incompatibilities of properties and relations do just this. But I argue from Combinatorialism to the Distinct-Existences Principle.

The principle, as we shall uphold it, may be stated thus:

> If A and B are wholly distinct existences, then it is possible for A to exist while no part of B does (and vice versa).

The principle applies straightforwardly to individuals, properties and relations. If the individuals do not overlap with each other, and if the universals lack any common constituent, then, for the Combinatorialist, it will always be possible for there to be a 'contracted' world which retains one individual but lacks any part of the other, or retains one universal while lacking any constituent of another. It is a further matter, of course, when we are and when we are not in the presence of wholly distinct existences.

With regard to states of affairs, to which the principle does *not* apply straightforwardly, we have already introduced the notion of their being 'Hume distinct'. This was intended to capture the notion of the states of affairs being distinct existences. In the universe as we originally conceived it, founded on *simple* individuals, properties and relations, all atomic states of affairs are Hume distinct. If we move to relative atoms, but keep the individuals without overlap, and the universals without common constituents, then the states of affairs that can be formed using these atoms are also Hume distinct from each other. If states of affairs are Hume distinct, then, for the Combinatorialist, we can have a possible world that is contracted by removing any one state of affairs without any other.

It is interesting to notice that the *converse* of Hume's principle also seems to be true:

> If it is possible for A to exist while no part of B does (and vice versa), then A and B are wholly distinct existences.

It is then illuminating to take the (logically equivalent) contrapositive of this Converse Principle:

If it is not the case that A and B are wholly distinct existences, then it is not possible for A to exist while no part of B does (and vice versa).

The Converse Principle now sounds rather Kripkean, although it covers more cases than Kripke's:

If A = B, then it is necessary that A = B.

Berent Enç pointed out to me that all this was anticipated by Hume in the *Treatise,* in unsatisfactory psychological guise:

We have observed, whatever objects are different are distinguishable, and that whatever objects are distinguishable are separable by the thought and imagination. And we may here add, that these propositions are equally true in the *inverse,* and that whatever objects are separable are also distinguishable, and that whatever objects are distinguishable are also different. For how is it possible we can separate what is not distinguishable, or distinguish what is not different? (Book I, Part I, Section VII)

The last sentence looks forward to Kripke.

V DISPOSITIONS, POWERS AND PROPENSITIES

The Distinct-Existences Principle forbids the existence of pure (i.e. non-categorical) dispositions and powers. Suppose that a has the disposition D to become E if it is acted on by a C in suitable circumstances. Let D be a non-relational property of a, but let us suppose that it is also thought of as a pure disposition or power. It is then of the essence of D that if something has D, and that something has suitable relational properties (is acted on by a C in suitable circumstances), then it becomes E. D might be brittleness conceived of as a non-categorical or pure disposition, C be being suitably struck and E be breaking.

Suppose now that a is suitably struck. Given that a has D, then it logically must break. But a's having D is a wholly distinct state of affairs from a's subsequent breaking. This is forbidden by the Distinct-Existences Principle, and so equally by Combinatorialism. Hence, for the Combinatorialist, D will have to be some categorical property of a, connected with the breaking, E, only by laws of nature (which are contingent).

Suppose, however, that D is a mere pure *propensity* to break. D is now still not categorical, but, whatever the circumstances, there is

117

no better than a chance that is less than 1 that *a* will break. The link between D and breaking is irreducibly probabilistic. Such a D might seem to be compatible with the Distinct-Existences Principle because there is no necessary connection between *a*'s having D and *a*'s breaking in suitable circumstances.

Nevertheless, there is a quasi-necessary connection involved, a sort of logical probability *in re*. And I think that a Combinatorialist must reject such a D. All the combinations may still be possible, including the world where Ds are given every opportunity to break by being struck but fail to break. Such a world may be indefinitely improbable, however, and not improbable by virtue of contingent laws of nature but by virtue of D alone. This reaching out by D to affect the probability of outcomes seems to run clear against the Combinatorial spirit.

For the Combinatorialist, then, all properties (and relations) are categorical properties. There are no *pure* dispositions, powers or propensities.

The position may be stated in terms of supervenience. If D is taken as a categorical property, then *a*'s brittleness is supervenient on the fact that *a* has D, together with the laws of nature that ensure that, in suitable circumstances, an *a* that has D breaks. Since the laws of nature connect wholly distinct things (properties), they are contingent. So in some other possible worlds *a* can have D, but not break, because the laws in those worlds are not those of the actual world. It seems linguistically permissible (but not compulsory) to identify D with the disposition, power or propensity. But it will be seen from the preceding that the identification is contingent.

Now, *a*'s having D, together with the appropriate laws of the actual world, is not supervenient on *a*'s being brittle. But *a*'s having D may not even be supervenient on the appropriate laws holding plus *a*'s being brittle. For we must allow for the epistemic possibility that *a* could lack D but have some other property, D', which would play the same role as D with regard to breaking when struck. That is, the laws may fail to ensure a type-type identification of D with brittleness.

9

Mathematics

In this chapter I sketch a view of mathematics which seems to go along harmoniously with a Combinatorialist Naturalism. We may distinguish, in routine manner, between mathematical *entities* and mathematical *truths*. The numbers 7, 5 and 12 are mathematical entities. That $7 + 5 = 12$ is a mathematical truth. Let us begin with a discussion of the nature of mathematical truth.

The first point I want to make about the truths of mathematics is a traditional one: that mathematical results are arrived at *a priori*. This is not a very popular position at the present time. I believe that this is because the notion of the *a priori* carries a theoretical loading derived from past centuries, a loading that is objectionable. But this loading can be removed without great difficulty, leaving a workable concept of the *a priori*. It is plausible to think that the truths of mathematics are *a priori* in this purged sense.

The loadings that need to be removed from the notion of the *a priori* are the notions of *certainty (a fortiori*, the Cartesian notion of *indubitable* or *incorrigible* certainty) and *knowledge*.

One philosopher who has moved in this direction is Kripke, who said,

Something can be known, or at least rationally believed, *a priori*, without being quite certain. You've read a proof in the math book; and, though you think it's correct, maybe you've made a mistake. You often do make mistakes of this kind. You've made a computation, perhaps with an error. (1980, p. 39)

Here Kripke seems to be thinking of the *a priori* as a process of arriving at belief, a process that will regularly but not invariably yield knowledge. I think this is the way to go.

This passage is quoted by Philip Kitcher (1983, p. 43), who agrees that in the case given by Kripke 'a non-empirical process engenders belief'. But he will not account the belief an *a priori* one. His reason seems to be that the product of the process is not believed with absolute reliability, that is to say, not *known*. But that, I suggest, is to adopt (or rather remain with) an unhelpful conception of the *a priori*.

Again, in a book by Patrick Suppes (1984) we find the following argument against an *a priori* conception of mathematics: 'If the truths of mathematics are known *a priori,* it seems absurd to find that corrections to mathematical articles are more prevalent than corrections to articles in any other domain of science' (p. 77). Suppes's observation is interesting, but why should he think it shows that mathematics is not *a priori?* I think the answer is clear. Suppes is assuming that there is a link between what is known *a priori* and our being certain of its truth. Only if that is his assumption can we explain why he thinks the prevalence of correction shows that mathematical truth is not known *a priori*.

But I should say, rather, that what his observation shows is that it is easy to think we have achieved *a priori* knowledge while actually having done no better than reached a mathematical belief *a priori*.

What, then, should be meant by saying that mathematical reasoning is *a priori?* Simply, I suggest, that it proceeds *solely* on the basis of thought and calculation and so not *a posteriori,* not on the basis of observation. (Computing is calculation, of course, even if *unsurveyable* calculation.)

Very often, the reward for those who make a concession is that they are asked to make still more. Many contemporary Empiricists feel the *a priori* is beyond salvaging. Once the Cartesian *a priori* is abandoned, it is best to recognize that there is no fundamental difference between natural science and mathematics.

Perhaps their strongest argument is the following line of thought. We need first to distinguish, as we have not so far distinguished, between mathematical *results* and mathematical *premisses*. The former are arrived at on the basis of mathematical proofs, and these are, or could be reconstructed as, deductively valid arguments. But here we need to concentrate on the premisses. These divide into two classes in turn. First, there are the epistemically original premisses, those propositions from which mathematical investigation begins. Second, there are those axioms which mathematicians use as axioms for their deductive systems.

The two classes of premisses do no more than overlap. For instance, '1 + 1 = 2' is about as epistemically fundamental as any mathematical proposition. But in the logistic system of *Principia Mathematica* it is a mere theorem, and one not quickly derived. Contrariwise, axioms may be chosen that are not at all obvious.

As Russell often stressed (Irvine, 1989), axioms are regularly chosen because of their consequences, that is, by their capacity to yield known mathematical truth, in particular epistemically original truth, plus perhaps interesting further consequences. Hence the adoption of an axiom or set of axioms is far more like inference to the best explanation than a process of being struck by apparent self-evidence.

And now it seems that all an empiricist about mathematics has to do is to claim, with Mill and others, that the epistemically prior mathematical premises are truths derived from observation, no different from the elementary truths of observation from which natural science begins. Mathematics, he may say then, is just a peculiarly general natural science. The start is from certain observed truths. Sets of axioms are postulated, just as in the paradigm natural sciences hidden laws or mechanisms are postulated which explain (and perhaps, in a degree correct) the original observations. Deductive development from the axioms may be compared with deductions from the postulated laws and/or mechanisms.

It seems to me, however, that to draw out this comparison is to see that it fails. When deductions are made from postulations in natural science, the process has not ended but has only begun. The essential further step is to check by observation (interlaced with theory) whether the matters deduced are or are not so. Then, and only then, are the deduced propositions taken to be true and the original postulations confirmed.

Nothing like this occurs in mathematics. There it is the deductions that need to be checked, not what is deduced nor what it is deduced from. What is deduced is not in general tested by observation, nor is it generally used to confirm the axiom-set from which it is deduced. This brings me back to the point that mathematics proceeds by thought and calculation almost exclusively. And it suggests quite strongly, what I believe to be true, that the epistemically primitive mathematical knowledge is *a priori* knowledge. I make the same concession Kant makes. That is, such truths may be suggested by experience. Still, our corrigible but considerable assurance of their truth is not grounded in experience.

The general situation in mathematics is to be *contrasted*, not compared, with the establishing of results in the natural sciences. Scientific method inspires great confidence, and rationally so. But the degree of certainty achieved is lower than that achieved in mathematics. I do not think that this lower degree of certainty springs very much from unreliability in observations. These unreliabilities can be allowed for. Still less does it spring from philosophical doubts about inductive methods. The real troubles are, first, that while some observation is reliable, there are invariably limits to its precision. As a result, the natural sciences involve approximation in a way that is not present in mathematical proof. Second, scientific theories are more entangled with each other than is the case with mathematical theories. Scientific theories have, to coin a phrase, a great tendency to face the tribunal of experience in large bodies (like terrorists on trial), which makes it more difficult to sort out true theories from false ones. In this respect, observation, though very compelling, is *less* compelling than mathematical proof.

It is the epistemic *superiority* of mathematical argument over the considerations adduced in the natural sciences which leads to the prevalence of corrections to mathematical articles, the prevalence to which Suppes draws attention. A putative result in mathematics is epistemically more secure than a result in the natural sciences. The mathematician can more easily dot 'i's and cross 't's because he has a much better chance of spotting the undotted or uncrossed 'i's or 't's than the scientist has. Precision can be sought because precision can be obtained.

So by adopting a relatively modest, anti–Cartesian, notion of the *a priori* we have defended the idea that mathematics is a purely (or almost purely) *a priori* discipline.

What conclusion can we draw from this conclusion concerning the nature of mathematical truth? There is now a huge corpus of mathematical knowledge and rational belief. How is it possible that we should have so much *a priori* knowledge? Hartry Field (1980) has argued that mathematics is not true at all. If that position is correct, then the question falls away. But I take the suggestion that mathematics is not (for the greatest part) true to be a fairly desperate one. Another view that might be taken is that the fundamental principles of mathematics are *a priori* because they are innate, with the rest of mathematics deduced from these principles. This explanation falters when it is remembered that innate propositions need not be true. Innate false belief is certainly possible, and might even be biologically advantageous in some circumstances. There are *useful* false beliefs. But, as already argued, we do not use deduction in mathematics to test the premises of our argument. Rather, we just detach what is deduced and add it to the corpus of supposed mathematical knowledge.

I suggest that the true explanation of our having so much *a priori* mathematical knowledge is that the truths of mathematics are *analytic*. They are established solely by reference to the content of the concepts involved, or the meanings of the symbols used to state the analytic truth, with at most the aid of elementary principles of logic.

Many mathematical results have a certain characteristic emptiness. Richard Feynman noted the tendency of mathematicians, once they have proved a result, to think of it as 'trivial' (1985, pp. 84–7). The emptiness is plausibly explained if the truths arrived at are analytic. On the other hand, the word 'trivial' must not be allowed to mislead. Analytic truth is not transparent truth. Knowledge of analytic truth is no more incorrigible or self-certifying or certain, or to be gained without intellectual struggle and effort and doubt, than knowledge of any other sort of truth.

If the truths of mathematics are analytic, then they are necessary. Now, in general, necessary truths have the form of hypothetical truths: if p, then q. It is plausible that this holds, again in general, for mathematical truths. '$7 + 5 = 12$' may be rendered as 'If there are seven things and five further things, then these things are just twelve things'. It may be said that '$7 + 5 = 12$' in addition asserts or presupposes the existence of the entities 7, 5 and 12. We shall, however, discuss assertions of the existence of mathematical entities in the next section, where a deflationary doctrine of mathematical existence will be offered. To say that the number 7 exists is to say no more than that it is possible that seven *things* should exist.

Consider now: 'If there are seven things and five further things, then these things are just twelve things'. If this is a necessary truth, then a thesis of *supervenience* will apply. In every possible world which contains seven things and five further things, then these things are just twelve things. The satisfaction of the consequent condition supervenes on the satisfaction of the antecedent condition. In this particular case, where we are dealing with an equality, the supervenience is symmetrical.

123

But it has been argued in this essay that what supervenes is not an ontological addition to what it supervenes on. The hypothetical truths of mathematics, then, require no more truth-maker than this: that the antecedent condition obtain. Indeed, even less than this is required. The antecedent condition need only obtain in some possible world.

So mathematical truth, it has been argued, is known *a priori,* is analytic and is necessary. But a word of caution may be appropriate. It is worth bearing in mind the example of Euclidean geometry. It was once thought to be a body of necessary truths which could be established by *a priori* argument on the basis of axioms whose own necessity could be directly apprehended. And in fact, given the axioms, then the further geometrical results can be shown to follow simply on the basis of general principles of reasoning. Geometries are deductive systems. But what we have known for some time now is that there is no necessity in at least some of the axioms. It is possible to deny some of the axioms without self-contradiction and adopt others. It is then a contingent question which set of axioms is true of space. In this way Euclidean geometry is broken down, on the one hand, into a purely mathematical portion where consequences are drawn *a priori* from axioms chosen with some freedom and, on the other, into a claim about the structure of space, a claim to be settled by natural science and, as it happens, a false claim.

Now it may be that this progress in purging mathematics of the contingent has not reached its end. For instance, the continuum hypothesis, the mathematical hypothesis that the number of the continuum is the *second* infinite cardinal, has been shown by Cohen to be undecidable. Whether or not it follows from the axioms of set theory depends on which axioms for set theory one adopts. Cohen has speculatively suggested that the continuum hypothesis is a contingent proposition whose truth is to be decided, if at all, by natural science (Cohen and Hersh 1967).

II MATHEMATICAL ENTITIES

After these remarks on mathematical truth, we may turn to the topic of mathematical entities. An obvious objection to Naturalism, the hypothesis that the space-time world is all there is, is that certain entities are admitted by mathematicians which may not have any existence in the natural world. For instance, for every infinite cardinal, there exists an infinite cardinal which is greater than it. It is very likely, then, that there exists an infinite cardinal which is greater than the number of things in the space-time world (unless we admit, for example, classes of any order among the things numbered, a move that looks very *ad hoc*). But if this infinite cardinal does not number anything in the space-time world, how can it exist in that world? Yet does not this infinite cardinal *exist?* Naturalism seems in danger.

It seems to me that the Combinatorial theory, as developed in this essay, contains within itself the resources to solve this difficulty. The theory allows not merely for the recombination of wholly distinct elements of the actual world, but also for the contraction of, *and expansion beyond,* the actual. The expansion does not extend to alien universals, but it does allow for the indefinite multiplication of individuals in a single possible world.

(I am here assuming that possible worlds can be constructed which contain an indefinite number of 'island universes' lying alongside each other, causally and spatio-temporally without connection yet part of the one world. My argument might be defeated if we allowed Lewis's contention that every possible world is, in some suitably broad sense, a spatio-temporal unity.)

But what has all this to do with the *existence* of mathematical entities? For us one-worlders, only one of the possible worlds exists. So what has the mere possibility of there being a certain infinite number of individuals in the universe to do with the *actual* existence of that cardinal number?

At this point in the argument the Combinatorial theory of possibility must be joined with an idea from the philosophy of mathematics. This is the not unfamiliar idea, put forward, for instance, by Hilary Putnam (1967), that, unlike natural science, mathematics concerns itself not so much with the actual as with the possible. In this view, mathematical existence is not really existence. A mathematical entity 'exists' if and only if there is no contradiction in the idea that things having this mathematical property should exist, that is, if and only if it is *possible* that things having this property exist. The infinite cardinals all 'exist' because it is possible, for each such cardinal, that the world should contain a collection of individuals or other entities whose number is that cardinal. It is important, and will be the business of the next section, to see how mathematical entities are anchored in actuality, but we must not expect that every mathematical concept is *directly* anchored in actuality.

This link between mathematical existence and possibility, if accepted, in turn reconfirms the view of mathematical truth already put forward in the preceding section. I argued that mathematical truths are known *a priori*, are analytic and are necessary. If, in mathematics, we gain knowledge about entities which in some cases are merely possible and, indeed, perhaps nomically impossible, then this knowledge must surely be a knowledge of necessary truths. Furthermore, there can be no question of establishing these conclusions *a posteriori*, as is the case with Kripkean necessities. These truths must be known *a priori*, if known at all.

But suppose further that we are not Realists about these possible worlds, instead thinking of them as *fictions*, made up in the sense that a story is made up, although governed in their constitution by certain Combinatorial principles. What can the ground of this *a priori* knowledge be? Not the merely possible worlds, which do not exist or subsist or have any sort of being. It is hard to see what that ground can be except the meanings of the terms with which we reason or, something that is presumably parallel to meanings, the structure of the concepts we employ. So mathematical truth will be analytic or conceptual truth.

One general thrust of the two preceding sections of this chapter has been to uphold a traditional idea. Mathematics, whether we are concerned with mathematical truths or mathematical entities, is concerned with a wider domain than that domain which it is the object of the natural sciences to describe and categorize. The natural sciences are concerned with the actual world. Mathematics is concerned with 'all possible worlds'.

III THE NATURE OF NUMBER

Mathematical 'existence', then, is the possibility of actual existence. But of what actual existences are we contemplating the possibility? Suppose that it is claimed that a certain number, identified by a certain mathematical description, exists. In the preceding section I said that if and only if there is a possible world which contains that number of individuals or other entities, then that number exists. But that hardly tells us what the numbers themselves are.

In this section I sketch a theory of the nature of number. (The

126

next section will offer a theory of what sets are.) It is greatly indebted to Peter Forrest, and is set out in greater detail in Forrest and Armstrong (1987). The theory has the advantage that it applies not only to the natural numbers, but also to the rational numbers, the reals and perhaps beyond. John Bigelow has brought it to our attention that the theory is really a revival of an old conception of number that became submerged in modern discussions.

According to this view, numbers are in the first place *internal relations between possible universals*. In particular, they are internal relations between a certain sort of possible *structural* universal and what I shall call a possible *unit-property*. (The qualification 'possible' is important for the reasons set out in the preceding section. But for ease of exposition I shall omit the qualification in future.) I believe that these internal relations between universals are the logically central cases of the numbers. But, as we will see, to get a comprehensive account of the use of the numerals, it will be necessary to move beyond universals to a much less strict conception of properties.

We begin, then, with the notion of a *strongly particularizing universal*. Such a universal is one that 'divides its extension', a phrase which is intended to echo Quine's semantic notion of an expression which 'divides its reference'. The instances of a universal which divides its extension are instances that do not overlap. If we consider the world of simple constituents with which we began in Chapter 3, then *being an F*, where *an* F is a simple individual, would be a strongly particularizing universal.

We now require the familiar distinction between a set and the aggregate that corresponds to that set. Suppose that there is a certain set of just nineteen electrons. Each electron is a member of the set. But each electron is also a part of a certain whole or aggregate constituted by the nineteen electrons. This whole or aggregate may be scattered in space and time. But it is a particular, having various properties, for instance a mass which is nineteen times that of an electron.

To any set to which a cardinal number can be attached there corresponds at most one such aggregate. But it is an important presupposition of this theory of number (as it is of the mereological calculus) that to each such set there corresponds at least one aggregate. Corresponding to the 'class as many' (the set of contemporary set theory) there is always a 'class as one'.

127

Now consider the whole or aggregate of the nineteen electrons. It has certain properties. In particular, it instantiates a certain structural universal, *being a nineteen-electron aggregate*.

Clearly there will be many other aggregate-universals of the same sort, all involving the number 19, for instance, *being a nineteen-proton aggregate*. One initially attractive idea is that the natural number 19 can be identified with a property, a higher-order property, which all these aggregate-universals have in common. In fact, however, this idea proves unworkable (see Forrest and Armstrong, Section I).

We now introduce the notion of a *unit-property*. For the case of natural numbers, unit-properties are universals of the same sort as their corresponding aggregate universal, but the aggregate-universal will bear a positive whole number ratio to its unit-property. For the universal *being a nineteen-electron aggregate* the (salient) unit-property is *being an electron,* and for *being a nineteen-proton aggregate* the (salient) unit-property is *being a proton*. Each of these pairs of universals, and innumerable other pairs of universals, bears the same (internal) relation to the others. The relation is a *ratio* or *proportion*. It is a plausible candidate, I suggest, for the natural number 19.

This links up with an old tradition. The following quotation from Newton's *Universal Arithmetick* (1769) was brought to my attention by John Bigelow:

> By *Number* we understand not so much a Multitude of Unities, as the abstracted Ratio of any *Quantity,* to another Quantity of the same kind, which we take for Unity. (p. 2)[1]

The 'Quantity . . . which we take for Unity' may be identified with what I have called a unit-property.

So on this view *being a nineteen-F aggregate* bears the 19 proportion to *being an F* and *being an aleph$_0$-F aggregate* bears the aleph$_0$ proportion to *being an F*. These proportions are identified with the numbers 19 and aleph$_0$, respectively. As a matter of fact, this account of the natural numbers will require a little supplementation. But ignoring that point for the present, one great interest of this

---

1 Frege mentions this view of Newton's in the *Grundlagen* (1884), Section 19. He takes Newton to be proposing a *geometrical* account of numbers, however. Frege also accuses the Newtonian definition of falling into circularity, although not, apparently, with great confidence in the charge.

view is that it generalizes to yield a unified account of the natural, the rational and the real numbers, and perhaps other species of numbers also.

Suppose we take *being one kilogram mass* as a unit-property. We can then take *being 2.5 kilograms mass* as standing in the 2.5 proportion to this unit. We can also take *being π kilograms in mass* as standing in the π proportion to the unit. Following Peter Forrest, in particular, we can identify these proportions with the rational number 2.5 and the real number π. This is an immense simplification over the current orthodoxy, where the naturals, the rationals and the reals are taken to be numbers *in different senses*. Notice, however, that in these cases we do not need to speak of aggregate-universals of the sort involved in the account of *natural* number. This points to an extra complication in the case of the natural numbers.

Contrast all this with a neo-Fregean account of natural number. Here a property (only a universal in rare cases) picks out a set of particulars. The particulars are all and only the objects having that property. (This makes such properties quite different from our unit-properties.) This set will have a certain number of members: nineteen say. There will be other properties which pick out sets having the same number of members. Then consider the set of all these 'nineteen' properties. The natural number *19* is taken to be a higher-order property possessed by all and only the members of this set of properties.

But attractive as this account is in some ways, it has the disadvantage that it will not generalize to the rational and the reals. They will have to be taken to be numbers in some further sense or senses.

The 'relation of proportion' account has what I think is another advantage over the neo-Fregean account. On the latter account, that a certain property has the 19 property will, in general, be a contingent matter. But the relation that holds, for example, between *being a nineteen-F aggregate* and *being an F* – the 19 proportion – is an internal relation. As such it is supervenient on its terms, thus, as we have argued, involving no ontological cost. In addition, such relations may be determined to hold *a priori*. We may connect and explain the 'powerlessness of numbers', their appearing to be above the flux, with this internality and supervenience.

If we consider an individual A, which is an aggregate of just nineteen Fs, *and if we abstract from the properties of A,* then it bears a relation to *being an F* which could also be identified with some plausibility as the number 19. Kessler (1980), who in some respects anticipates the Forrest–Armstrong view, makes just this identification. This relation would be contingent. But it is clear that this relation holds *in virtue of* A's aggregate-property. The latter property is the ground of the contingent relation. And so, because the aggregate-property provides the ground, the internal relation that holds between it and the unit-property seems the natural relation to identify the number 19 with, rather than the Kessler relation.

I have sketched the view of number as ratio or proportion as a relation between universals. But having done so we need to extend the relation to properties that are not universals: disjunctive properties, negative properties and properties involving particulars (being a horse *of the king's*). The reason why we must admit such properties is that the unit-properties, in terms of which the number-proportion holds, regularly involve such properties. Consider, for instance, the number of persons in the room who are either bald or toothless. The unit-property involves essential reference to particulars, disjunction and negation: *person in the room who lacks either hair or teeth*.

I do not think there is any reason to worry about this extension. We saw in the preceding chapter that such properties are supervenient on first-order states of affairs involving universals, or, in the case of negative properties, such states of affairs together with second-order states of affairs in addition. The internal relations between these unit properties and the corresponding aggregate-properties are likewise supervenient. The sloppy nature of the unit-properties and the aggregate-properties correspond in each case, cancelling out and producing the same internal proportion-relations that we find in the case of universals.

I now try to show what is special about the *natural* numbers, as opposed to the rationals and the reals. (Here I may differ from Forrest.) The relationship between *being 2.5 kilograms in mass* and *being one kilogram in mass* is just a single thing – the number 2.5. It is true that there are innumerable ways of dividing something of 2.5 kilograms in mass into two objects each of one kilogram plus one object of half a kilogram. But that seems irrelevant to the relation of proportion which holds between the two mass-universals.

But the natural numbers do involve something more than a proportion. The additional factor is this. We have an aggregating property (say, *made up of just nineteen electrons*) and a unit-property (say, *being an electron*). The aggregating property is instantiated by a certain particular, the aggregate. The unit-property operates on the aggregate to produce *without remainder* at least one set, where each member of such a set has the unit-property. (What a set is will be the business of the next section.) Newton's *first* (and played-down) phrase applies to this set or sets: Each is a 'Multitude of Unities'. No such sets are involved in the proportions that constitute the rational and the real numbers, except for those rationals and reals that are also natural numbers.

It is important to note the point just made: that the unit-property may operate on the aggregate that instantiates the aggregating property to produce (without remainder) *more* than one set whose members each instantiate the unit-property. If the aggregating property is *made up of just eighteen electrons* (= *made up of just nine two-electron aggregates*) and the unit property is *made up of just two electrons,* then it is easy to see that the unit-property as it were carves up the aggregating property to give a large number of different sets.

Up to this point we have worked solely with strongly particularizing universals, ones that 'divide their extension'. But consider the following diagram (which is to be taken as a type rather than a token) introduced by Peter Simons (1982):

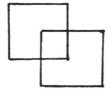

Simons asks how many marked-off squares the diagram contains. The problem for what has been said so far is this: Suppose we insist that unit-properties must divide their extension. Then the only answer that we can give to Simons's question is 'just one', although there are three different objects that could be that one. But much more natural answers are 'two' or 'three'. These answers, however, require a unit-property (different for the two answers) which does *not* divide its extension.

Why should we not simply accept unit-properties that do not divide their extensions? As a matter of fact, we could accept Simons's case. But the trouble is that other cases can then easily be constructed using this relaxed sort of unit-property where the relation of unit-property to aggregating property becomes numerically thoroughly ambiguous.

Let the unit-property be *made up of just one million atoms of lead*. Let the aggregating property be *made up of just one thousand million atoms of lead*. If the unit-property divides its extension, then the single proportion of *one thousand* emerges. We can live with the fact that there are innumerable ways of dividing the thousand million into just a thousand particulars, each particular non-overlapping with the others, and each made up of just a million atoms of lead.

But suppose that the unit-property does not necessarily divide its extension. For any particular 'carve-up' of the aggregating property by the unit-property different proportions emerge, *and so no definite number can be assigned*. The internal relationships between the two properties are still there, but they are much less interesting and salient, and involve a disjunction of numbers.

The situation becomes even more chaotic if unit-properties are admitted that involve disjunctions and negations of universals, and also particulars (*horse of the king's*). We have already said just a little while ago that they cannot be excluded as unit-properties. But if they are in addition such that they fail to divide their extension, then a chaotic result follows in many cases.

The result is, I think, that it is reasonable to treat such cases as the Simons diagram as secondary cases of number. The concept is being extended, reasonably happily in the Simons case, but less happily in other cases which use unit-properties that fail to divide their extension.

It remains to say something about those special numbers 1 and 0. In the case of 1, the unit-property and the aggregate-property are the very same property. So the 1 relation will have to be the (internal and supervenient) relation to *identity*. I think this consequence of the theory is natural enough. The notions of one and of identity are clearly closely connected. Everything is automatically identical with itself, and everything is one.

As for 0, one may suggest this: Given a unit-property and given an aggregating property to which the unit-property *lacks* numerical relation of any sort, then the two properties stand in the 0 relation. It is true that the ontology we have adopted makes no place for negative universals so that the 0 relation cannot be a universal. But since the relation is internal (like the relation of difference) we do not have to treat it with too much ontological seriousness. Given the two positive terms of the relation – the two properties – then we have the 0 relation.

It is interesting to see that the Kessler relations – those holding between a unit-property and a token aggregate as opposed to a property – will offer us a version of the 0 relation. The aggregate will lack any property which would be an aggregating property for that unit-property. The truth-maker for this, given my treatment of negation (Chapter 7, Section II), will be the state of affairs of the aggregate having the (positive) properties that it has, together with the higher-order state of affairs that these properties are the totality of the properties of the aggregate-object.

I add a final point. It would be possible to substitute for the relations of proportion with which I have identified numbers (with an additional element for the case of the natural numbers), a *relational property* of the aggregating property. Oxford blue has the internal relation of *being darker in colour than* Cambridge blue. So it has the relational property of *being darker in colour than Cambridge blue*. Similarly, *being an aggregate of nineteen Fs* stands in the internal relation which we have identified as 19 to *being an F*. But equally the aggregate universal has the relational property of *having the 19 relation to being an F*. If one wishes to maintain the intuition that numbers are properties rather than relations, then here is a candidate for a property provided for from inside the theory. Of course, the one aggregate-universal may have, in general will have, other such relational properties as well: perhaps, for instance, *having the 38-relation to being a half-F*. But a particular relational property together with a particular unit-property may well be salient in the actual situation that is being considered.

IV SETS

Philosophers have not found it easy to sort out sets from aggregates. Suppose, then, that we have an aggregate $[a + b + c \ldots]$. What will transform it into the corresponding set $\{a, b, c, \ldots \}$? If $a, b, c, \ldots$ are individuals (first-order particulars), then their aggregate is also an individual. Sets are also particulars, because unlike universals they are not repeatables; they are not ones that run through many. But a set of individuals, though a particular, is not an individual.

In a set the disjunction among its members is emphasized, perhaps preparatory to saying something about each one of them by means of the distributive 'all'. In an aggregate the bringing together of its parts is emphasized, perhaps preparatory to saying something about the whole by means of the collective 'all' ('the class as many *versus* the class as one'). The special nature of the set, and the distinction of its members, would be done justice to if we embedded each member-individual in a *state of affairs,* and then, for a plural set, conjoined these states of affairs to give a conjunctive state of affairs. These states of affairs are not repeatable, and so they are particulars. Sets, then, are *states of affairs.*

If this is on the right track, then the next question is how we are to select the properties of the individuals in order to make up the states of affairs in which each individual is to be embedded. A first restriction seems plausible. Each property must be such that we can speak of *an* F, *a* G, and so forth. They must particularize the individuals which instantiate them. Only so do we preserve the link with *units* and *number* that is part of the essence of a set.

Given this restriction, what then? One thing to do would be to select every particularizing property of every member of the set, including under the heading of 'properties' relational properties and even properties that are not universals (although the last-named would be supervenient). These properties could then all be conjoined. But it would seem to come closer to the Idea of a set to *disjoin* them, thus producing a disjunctive property with many disjuncts (a property supervenient on the conjunction, however) for each individual to instantiate.

However, it seems desirable, at least, to take the properties that figure in the disjunctions to be properties possessed by *each* member of the set. The classical, Fregean-Russellian, way of doing this would be to use those particularizing properties which are necessary *and sufficient* for an individual to be a member of the set. One could then assign to each member the very same disjunctive property – the disjunction of all such properties. It is to be noted that in this way of doing things very few sets would have universals among the disjuncts. (The only such sets would be those whose members are all and only the instances falling under a certain universal.)

The idea involved here that the members of a set should each be embedded in states of affairs involving a disjunction of exactly the same properties seems a good one. It pays tribute to the idea that, at least in some minimal sense, a set is a unified affair. I think, however, that it is actually enough if the properties in question are *necessary* for an individual to be a member of that set. We are then including the unit-properties that I spoke of in the preceding section, and if the speculations on number in that section are correct, the link between natural number and set is reflected by these properties. The aggregate that is the sum of the members of the set will in each case have aggregate-properties that correspond to the unit-properties, and the relation of proportion between these two properties gives the number of the members of the set.

But I should add that I do not think the matter of just what properties of the individuals are admitted in constructing sets is a vital one. Perhaps the decision is somewhat arbitrary. The important thing is that each individual should be embedded in a state of affairs. In that way the individuals in plural sets are split up from each other ('the class as many') instead of coalescing into a single aggregate ('the class as one').

We are, however, left with a problem about higher-order particulars. First-order particulars ('individuals') all have properties and stand in relations to other individuals, properties and relations that are universals. But first-order particulars are not the only things that can be members of sets. Universals can be members, indeed any entity at all can be. But an *a posteriori* realism about universals can have no confidence, to put it mildly, that all these entities instantiate universals. But in that case, are they embedded in states of affairs?

In the preceding chapter we admitted properties and relations in a relaxed sense, however, and, with these, states of affairs in a relaxed sense. They are supervenient on the 'strict' states of affairs, which later we take to be the true joints of reality. As a result, I think it will be enough to give a member of a set a property (which may be a relational property) in a relaxed sense of 'property'. All that is required, I suggest, is that some *description* be contingently true of the set member. This will yield a relaxed property and, with it, relaxed states of affairs. Some 'strict' state of affairs, in some way involving the individual, will then be the truth-maker for the description. It seems reasonable to think that this demand for a contingent description can always be met.

A number of other issues now require brief discussion: higher-order sets (including higher-order unit-sets), ordered sets (ordered *n*-tuples) and the null class.

Higher-order sets. Suppose that a number of first-order sets are collected as members of a second-order set. How shall we construct the required state of affairs? Consider one of the first-order sets. It will be a complex state of affairs. Perhaps it is *a* is (P∨Q . . .) and *b* is (P∨Q . . .) and *c* is (P∨Q . . .). Now we can abstract from *a, b* and *c*, substituting unbound variables, and reach the conception of the *type* of state of affairs of which this is a token. Do the same for the other sets which are members of the second-order set. We will have a number of types of states of affairs. Disjoin these types and we have a still more complex disjunctive type. Because it is a type, it is a property that is instantiated by *each* state of affairs that constitutes each of the first-order sets. So it is a property common to each member of the higher-order set. As a result, we can exhibit the higher-order set as a higher-order state of affairs, involving a conjunction of states of affairs where the conjuncts are the first-order sets. It will not matter that these states of affairs supervene on first-order states of affairs; indeed, that is what we want, because higher-order sets supervene on their members.

Consider now unit-sets. To place the individual *a* into a set {*a*} is to embed *a* in a state of affairs. So how do we interpret {{*a*}}? It will be something very empty: the state of affairs of a certain state of affairs obtaining. I do not think we need to worry about this emptiness. Does it not reflect the emptiness of the operation which places {*a*} in a unit-set?

Ordered n-*tuples.* What is an ordered set, on this view? It is in the first place a set, and so a conjunction of states of affairs. What is needed is something which will order the individuals that figure in the conjunct states of affairs, or the states of affairs themselves, correlating them with the integers. This correlation will be a *relation,* of course. It could well be an internal relation. The first member of the *n*-tuple will have a certain relation to 1, the second a *different* relation to 2, and so on. These relations automatically generate *relational properties: having R_1 to 1, having R_2 to 2* . . . which attach to the successive members of the *n*-tuple. These relational properties give the order. Of course, the *n*-tuple must have the usual extensionality. To achieve this *having R_1 to 1* is expanded into a disjunction of *all* those Rs to 1 which put the first member of the n-tuple first, and so up to R_n.

The null class. What finally of the null class? A non-existent thing is not to be found anywhere or anywhen at all, although it may be 'found' in a possible world. Consider, then, all those possible properties which would pick out some particular if they were actual properties, but which in fact pick out none. That their disjunction fails to be true of any particular at all is a negative existential state of affairs. It appears to be the null class: Nothing is unicornish or centaurish or . . . The truth-maker for this, what it is supervenient on, will be the conjunction of all the states of affairs in the strict sense, plus all higher-order states of affairs. These *are* all the states of affairs.

10

Final questions: logic

Finally, what of the logical truths? They are necessary, it seems. But can we give an account of such things in terms of our possible worlds?

The problem we face here is part of a more general problem. I postulated a certain structure for the world which yields a certain theory of possibility, and I reasoned about this structure. Possibility was defined using that structure. But if so, what of the status of the postulation and of the theory and, again, the principles of reasoning used in their development? Are they to be taken as necessary truths? If they are necessary, how are they to be brought within the scope of my theory?

If my theory, including my theory of possible worlds, is true, then no exception will be found to the theory in any possible world, thus making the theory necessary. But this seems trivial. If that is all that there is to the necessity of the theory, it does not seem very necessary.

Consider a concrete instance: I postulated a world of states of affairs having individuals and universals as constituents. The constituents, I argued, cannot appear outside states of affairs. But what is the status of this prohibition? Why must it hold 'in every possible world'?

Again, in defending the theory I had to reason about it. I pointed out what I take to be its consequences – for instance, that it forbids alien universals in other possible worlds. What is the status of the reasoning involved? In drawing consequences, I was deducing. But what is the status of the principles of deduction thus tacitly employed? It seems natural to treat these principles as necessary truths. But given the general theory they are used to develop, what is the force of calling them necessary?

Faced with this problem, I say three things:

First, it may be that many of the statements made, and the principles employed, can plausibly be said to be *analytic*. I now mean this word in its strongest sense: true *solely* by virtue of the meanings of the symbols employed in the statement (while allowing that the *establishment* of sameness of meaning may be a matter of great difficulty and delicacy). Consider, for instance, the claim made in Chapter 3 that by 'property' should be meant 'ways particulars are' and by 'relation' should be meant 'ways individuals stand to each other'. *If* these are correct definitions (I pass over the truly delicate question of how to establish this antecedent), then it is analytic that properties and relations demand particulars to instantiate them. And, it would seem, analyticity of this strong sort yields necessity *without* appeal to Combinatorial theory.

Consider, again, the fundamental logical principle *modus ponens*. It does not seem a far-fetched claim, and I think it is a true one, that it flows from the *very meaning* of 'if . . . then . . .' that *modus ponens* holds.

Second, we may have to accept that, concerning the fundamental theory of the world, much of what we say is *neither* necessary nor contingent, but simply true or false. The fundamental and pervasive nature of such truths, if they are true, may be what helps to create the illusion that they are necessarily true. Where necessity and contingency are analysed by means of a certain theory, the Combinatorial theory, then the price that may have to be paid is the denial that the theory itself is either necessary or contingent. I do not think the price is too high.

Third, there is a fall-back position, for which I am indebted to David Lewis (1986a, p. 156 para. 4). My hope is that the Combinatorial theory has given us a reductive analysis of possibility and necessity. In this view, to be possible, in particular, is simply to put together wholly distinct constituents from states of affairs in a way that does not always respect actuality, but does respect the structure of states of affairs. It may be, however, that the analysis is covertly circular and that the theory itself makes use of the very notion of modality that it is intended to analyse.

If this turns out to be so, as I hope it does not, then my suggestion is that what I have been giving in this essay is not an *analysis* of possibility and necessity but, rather, something more modest. It would merely be an attempt to exhibit in a perspicuous manner the *structure* of modality, a structure (as I have claimed) of no great complexity. I do not like the idea that modality is a fundamental, unanalysable feature of actuality. In particular, I see great epistemological problems for a Naturalist in explaining the process by which we come to know of the existence of such features of actuality. Nevertheless, if things go badly for my argument, the unanalysability of modality may just have to be accepted. But this acceptance would not absolve us from the attempt to systematize and organize the theory of the unanalysable modal data. This essay could then be seen as an attempt to do no more than provide such a theory.

Even a modal realist such as Lewis could largely accept my Combinatorial view as an account of the structure of the other worlds. He would have to accept universals, about which he is doubtful. He would, if he accepted the ontological primacy of the actual, have to reject genuinely alien universals. But that is all. And of course, if in unconvenanted addition he were then to turn fictionalist about the other worlds, he would have arrived at a Combinatorial Naturalism.

Works cited

Adams, R. 1974. 'Theories of Actuality'. *Nous*, 8. Reprinted in *The Possible and the Actual*. Ed. M. J. Loux. Ithaca, N.Y., Cornell University Press, 1979.

Anscombe, G. E. M. 1971. *Causality and Determination*. Cambridge, Cambridge University Press. Reprinted in *Causation and Conditionals*. Ed. E. Sosa. Oxford, Oxford University Press, 1975.

Armstrong, D. M. 1968. 'The Headless Woman and the Defence of Materialism'. *Analysis*, 29:48–9.

Armstrong, D. M. 1978a. *Nominalism and Realism*. Vol. 1 of *Universals and Scientific Realism*. Cambridge, Cambridge University Press.

Armstrong, D. M. 1978b. *A Theory of Universals*. Vol. 2 of *Universals and Scientific Realism*. Cambridge, Cambridge University Press.

Armstrong, D. M. 1980. 'Against "Ostrich" Nominalism: A Reply to Michael Devitt'. *Pacific Philosophical Quarterly*, 61: 440–9.

Armstrong, D. M. 1983. *What Is a Law of Nature?* Cambridge, Cambridge University Press.

Armstrong, D. M. 1986. 'The Nature of Possibility'. *Canadian Journal of Philosophy*, 16: 575–94.

Armstrong, D. M. 1987. 'Smart and the Secondary Qualities'. In *Mind, Morality and Metaphysics: Essays in Honour of J. J. C. Smart*. Ed. P. Pettit, R. Sylvan and J. Norman. Oxford, Blackwell.

Armstrong, D. M. 1988. 'Are Quantities Relations?: A Reply to Bigelow and Pargetter'. *Philosophical Studies*, 54: 305–16.

Armstrong, D. M. 1989. *Universals*, Boulder, Colo., Westview Press.

Bigelow, J., and R. Pargetter. 1988. 'Quantities'. *Philosophical Studies*, 54: 287–304.

Boolos, G. 1971. 'The Iterative Conception of Set'. *Journal of Philosophy*, 68:215–31.

Bradley, R. 1989. 'Possibility and Combinatorialism: Wittgenstein Versus Armstrong'. *Canadian Journal of Philosophy*, 19.

Broad, C. D. 1933. *Examination of McTaggart's Philosophy*, vol. 1. Cambridge, Cambridge University Press.

Carnap, R. 1962. *Logical Foundations of Probability*. Chicago, University of Chicago Press.

Cohen, P. J., and R. Hersh. 1967. 'Non-Cantorian Set Theory'. *Scientific American*, 217: 104–17.

Cresswell, M. 1972. 'The World Is Everything That Is the Case'.

Australasian Journal of Philosophy, 50. Reprinted in *The Possible and the Actual*. Ed. M. J. Loux. Ithaca, N.Y., Cornell University Press, 1979.

Devitt, M. 1980. ' "Ostrich Nominalism" or "Mirage Realism" '. *Pacific Philosophical Quarterly*, 61: 433–9.

Feynman, R. P. 1985. *'Surely You're Joking, Mr Feynman!'* London, Unwin.

Field, H. 1980. *Science without Numbers*. Princeton, N.J., Princeton University Press.

Forrest, P., and D. M. Armstrong, 1984. 'An Argument against David Lewis' Theory of Possible Worlds'. *Australasian Journal of Philosophy*, 62:164–8.

Forrest, P., and D. M. Armstrong. 1987. 'The Nature of Number'. *Philosophical Papers*, 16: 165–86.

Frege, G. 1884. *Die Grundlagen der Arithmetik*. Translated by J. L. Austin as *The Foundations of Arithmetic*. Oxford: Blackwell, 1950.

Hume, D. *A Treatise of Human Nature*. Ed. L. A. Selby-Bigge. Oxford, Oxford University Press.

Irvine, A. D. 1989. 'Epistemic Logicism and Russell's Regressive Method'. *Philosophical Studies*, 55: 303–27.

Kessler, G. 1980. 'Frege, Mill and the Foundations of Arithmetic'. *Journal of Philosophy*, 77: 65–79.

Kim, J. 1986. 'Possible Worlds and Armstrong's Combinatorialism'. *Canadian Journal of Philosophy*, 16: 595–612.

Kitcher, P. 1983. *The Nature of Mathematical Knowledge*. Oxford, Oxford University Press.

Kripke, S. 1980. *Naming and Necessity*. Oxford, Blackwell.

Lewis, D. K. 1986a. *On the Plurality of Worlds*. Oxford, Blackwell.

Lewis, D. K. 1986b. 'Against Structural Universals'. *Australasian Journal of Philosophy*, 64: 25–46.

Lycan, W. G. 1979. 'The Trouble with Possible Worlds'. In *The Possible and the Actual*. Ed. M. J. Loux. Ithaca, N.Y., Cornell University Press.

Mellor, D. H. 1980. 'Necessities and Universals in Natural Laws'. In *Science, Belief and Behaviour*. Ed. D. H. Mellor. Cambridge, Cambridge University Press.

Millikan, R. G. 1984. *Language, Thought and Other Biological Categories*. Cambridge, Mass., Bradford Books.

Newton, I. 1769. *Universal Arithmetick*.

Perry, J., ed. 1975. *Personal Identity*. Berkeley, University of California Press.

Putnam, H. 1967. 'The Thesis that Mathematics Is Logic'. In *Bertrand Russell, Philosopher of the Century*. Ed. R. Shoenman. London, Allen & Unwin. Reprinted in Putnam, *Mathematics, Matter and Method: Philosophical Papers*, vol. I. Cambridge, Cambridge University Press.

Quine, W. V. 1969. 'Propositional Objects'. In Quine, *Ontological Relativity and Other Essays*. New York, Columbia University Press.

Quine, W. V. 1980. 'Soft Impeachment Disowned'. *Pacific Philosophical Quarterly*, 61: 450–1.

142

Ramsey, F. P. 1925. 'Universals'. Reprinted in *Foundations*. Ed. D. H. Mellor. London, Routledge & Kegan Paul, 1978.

Russell, B. 1903. *The Principles of Mathematics*. London, Allen & Unwin.

Russell, B. 1918. *The Philosophy of Logical Atomism*. Ed. D. Pears. London, Fontana/Collins, 1972.

Russell, B. 1948. *Human Knowledge, Its Scope and Limits*. London, Allen & Unwin.

Seargent, D. 1985. *Plurality and Continuity*. The Hague, Martinus Nijhoff.

Shoemaker, S. 1984. *Identity, Cause & Mind*. Cambridge, Cambridge University Press.

Simons, P. 1982. 'Against the Aggregate Theory of Number'. *Journal of Philosophy*, 79: 163–7.

Skyrms, B. 1981. 'Tractarian Nominalism'. *Philosophical Studies*, 40: 199–206.

Suppes, P. 1984. *Probabilistic Metaphysics*. Oxford, Blackwell.

Swoyer, C. 1982. 'The Nature of Natural Laws'. *Australasian Journal of Philosophy*, 60: 203–23.

Swoyer, C. 1983. 'Realism and Explanation'. *Philosophical Inquiry*, 5: 14–28.

Swoyer, C. 1987. 'The Metaphysics of Measurement'. In *Measurement, Realism and Objectivity*. Ed. J. Forge. Dordrecht, Reidel.

Williams, D. C. 1962. 'Dispensing with Existence'. *Journal of Philosophy*, 59: 748–63.

Williams, D. C. 1966. *Principles of Empirical Realism*. Springfield, Ill., Charles C. Thomas.

Williamson, T. 1985. 'Converse Relations'. *Philosophical Review*, 94: 249–62.

Wittgenstein, L. 1921. *Tractatus Logico-Philosophicus*. Trans. D. F. Pears and B. F. McGuiness. London: Routledge & Kegan Paul, 1961.

Appendix:
Tractarian Nominalism,
by Brian Skyrms

(for Wilfrid Sellars)[1]

In the *Tractatus* Wittgenstein sketches a metaphysical position which displays nominalistic sympathies although it is certainly not nominalistic in either the terms of Ockham, or those of Quine and Goodman.[2] In this note, I would like to explore a version of this position, and to say in what ways it is nominalistic and in what ways it is not. My aim is not, however, faithful exegesis of the *Tractatus*. The view which I call Tractarian Nominalism will have no part of Wittgenstein's interpretation of quantifiers, his fixed-domain treatment of possible worlds, or his quasi-intuitionist attitude towards infinity. Rather, I would like to give what I take to be the central idea of the *Tractatus* free play in less cramped quarters. The resulting metaphysics does, I believe, represent a viable ontological position. It has an advantage over traditional nominalism in the way in which it is connected to questions of epistemology. And it has an important consequence for the philosophy of logic.

Tractarian Nominalism:

Wittgenstein's truly daring idea was that the ontology of the subject (nominalism) and the ontology of the predicate (platonism) were both equally wrong and one-sided; and that they should give way to the ontology of the assertion. We may conceive of the

Philosophical Studies 40 (1981) 199–206. Copyright © 1981 by D. Reidel Publishing Co., Dordrecht, Holland, and Boston, U.S.A. Reprinted by permission.

1 The dedication is not to be taken as implying that Sellars is a Tractarian Nominalist; this note is not to be taken as implying that he is not.

2 Of 'Steps toward a constructive nominalism' and 'A world of individuals' but compare Quine's views in 'Whither physical objects?'

world not as a world of individuals or as a world of properties and relations, but as a world of facts – with individuals and relations being equally abstractions from the facts. John would be an abstraction from all facts-about-john; Red an abstraction from being-red-facts; etc.

Of course *in the metalanguage of the Tractatus,* facts became the objects named, and their properties and relations (being-a-fact-about-john; being-a-being-red-fact) assume the office of the first order objects and relations with which we started. If stated with no restrictions as to language, the metaphysics of the *Tractatus* is incoherent.[3] Wittgenstein chose to interpret his theory in the most grandiose way, and then bite the bullet by agreeing that the language of the *Tractatus* is nonsense. His show of facing up to the consequences by 'throwing away the ladder' is, however, hardly more than a bit of theater. It would be more satisfactory to take the modest position that what is being attempted is not a theory of all language but rather a theory of the functioning of the object language used to describe the world. Let us take this tack, and table the question as to what is going on in our metalanguage.

The world, then, can be thought of as a collection of facts. Facts are primitive entities. Nevertheless we can say something about their nature in terms of the way in which we classify them. An atomic fact can be completely characterized by a relational-classification (e.g. is-a-loves-fact) and its coordinate object-classifications (e.g. with John standing in the first place of the loving relation and Mary in the second). We may then, in the vulgar way, think of an atomic fact as associated with a representation consisting of a $n + 1$-tuple: an n-ary relation followed by n objects. But the representation need not be *unique.* ⟨Loves, John, Mary⟩ and ⟨is-Loved-by, Mary, John⟩ are representations of the same fact.

I see no just reason to maintain that n has to be finite. A relation associated with a fact might be a relation with an infinite number of terms. In such a case, 'n-tuple' in the foregoing should be interpreted as: 'family indexed by the ordinal n'. This raises the immediate prospect of a grand all embracing fact.

If it is a fact that John loves Mary and it is a fact that Jane desires George, and if we are allowed to infer from the two two-place

---

3 The most immediate incoherence being simply the consequence that facts are and are not objects.

relations of love and desire, a four place relation $Rxyzw$ which holds for $xyzw$ just in case x loves y and z loves w, then there is the fact that this relation is exemplified by ⟨John, Mary, Jane, George⟩. The most liberal attitude for closure conditions for relations will lead to the all encompassing world-fact.

Conversely, *if* we allow a property of being-the-son-of-Adam, or being-the-father-of-Cain, then the fact-that-Abel-is-the-son-of-Adam, i.e. that Adam-is-the-father-of-Cain, has not only the two representations:

⟨Child-of, Cain, Adam⟩
⟨parent of, Adam, Cain⟩

but also:

⟨child-of-Adam, Cain⟩
⟨parent-of-Cain, Adam⟩

So the world could be characterized by a set of monadic representations of facts.

Which level should we take as fundamental? Does it make any difference? First an epistemological point. The fact representations that we take as fundamental are co-ordinate with the objects and relations that we take as fundamental. The way we break things up depends on what objects and relations we take as being more *generally* useful in characterizing the world. This determination is made by *science*, not logic. [E.g. at a crude level of science greenness may be a fundamental property but grueness is not.] Science judges which are the fundamental objects and relations of the world. This is a *pragmatic* evaluation.

This determination affects the way we think about possibilities. Possible worlds are collections of compossible facts. We think about possible facts and possible worlds in two quite different ways. For possible worlds whose objects and relations are subsets of this world our possibilities are essentially *combinatorial*. We re-arrange some or all of our relationships between some or all of the objects to get our possibilities. It is possible for the mat to be on the cat. (Of course not all combinations count as possible – the mat cannot be larger than itself – but I think that it is still fair to say that the reasoning involved here is basically combinatorial.)[4]

4 I will not attempt here any account of how combinatorial possibility is so restricted.

The combinatorial economy which makes the fundamental predicates valuable for the scientist is reflected in our conception of possibility.

Wittgenstein believes that this is the *only* conception of possibility that we can have, and indeed that all possible worlds must contain exactly the same objects. I regard this restriction as inessential to Tractarian Nominalism, and indeed, as rather unfortunate.

There might be more, or other objects than there are. There might be other forces in nature, other physical properties and relations. To cash these intuitions we must think of possibilities *analogically*. There might be other things that play the role of our objects; other things that play the role of our relations.

For the Tractarian Nominalist, these two stages in the construction of possibilia are logically quite different. He takes both objects and relations quite seriously, and puts them on a par. Neither is reduced to the other. So in the combinatorial phase of the construction of possibilia, isomorphic possible worlds are regarded as *distinct!* There are genuinely different individuals standing in the same relations. At this stage of the game the Tractarian Nominalist is what David Kaplan calls a 'haecciatist'.

In the analogical phase, however, the game is quite different. Suppose that in addition to some objects and relations from our world, there are some 'new' objects a, b, c and some 'new' relations R_1, R_2, R_3. The only significance of these new blocks lies in their arrangement vis-à-vis each other and vis-à-vis the elements of the real world. A possible world made of 'other' new objects d, e, f and 'other' new relations R_5, R_6, R_7 arranged in the same way would not be a different world, but the same one. So at this stage, haecciatism fails, and a kind of Ramsey sentence (on the level of the models) approach to the 'new' elements prevails.

WHAT IS NOMINALISTIC ABOUT TRACTARIAN NOMINALISM?

In what sense is Tractarian Nominalism nominalism at all? It is certainly not nominalism in the sense of Goodman ['A world of individuals'] or Quine ['On what there is'], since it finds quantification over properties and relations of individuals just as acceptable as quantification over individuals, and cashes both in terms of facts.

But its properties and relations are all properties and relations *of*

148

individuals and its facts are all *first-order* facts: facts 'about' individuals. There are no higher-order facts: facts consisting of relations between relations and objects or relations between relations and relations. In particular, there are no causal relations between relations and individuals.

But can it be quite right to say that there are *no* higher order facts? If Socrates is wise then wisdom has the second order property of being instantiated, and indeed the second order property of being-instantiated-by-Socrates.

We can say that the-fact-that-wisdom-is-instantiated-by-Socrates is not really a second order fact but merely a redescription of the first order fact that Socrates is wise. There is no first-order atomic fact that can be described as the fact that wisdom is instantiated, but that wisdom is instantiated is *determined* by the first order atomic facts. What the Tractarian Nominalist means to deny then is that there are any *autonomous* higher order propositions. *What he means to deny is that there are two distinct possible worlds which share all the same first order facts.*[5] He will countenance only such higher order truths as are supervenient in this way on the first order facts.

Thus Tractarian Nominalism contrasts with the sort of free-swinging Tractarian Platonism which countenances all sorts of higher-order facts which are not so supervenient. (For example: someone who holds that we can perceive properties and relations, and that such perceptions need not reduce to relations between objects.)

Tractarian Nominalism is motivated by the view of science or epistemology that suggests that either we don't, or cannot, have evidence for such autonomous higher order facts. Here I think that Tractarian Nominalism makes contact with the epistemological wellsprings of nominalist thought; while Quine-Goodman nominalism can only appeal to philosophical conscience or taste.

TRACTARIAN-NOMINALISTIC LOGIC

To what sort of logic should a tractarian Nominalist subscribe? It has already been emphasized that he can make sense of all the sentences of second-order quantification theory. It should be appar-

---

5 This model theoretic sense of reducibility sets off the Tractarian nominalist from Bergman's 'Elementarist', who holds quite a different thesis.

ent that second order quantification theory with the usual quantifier rules is *sound* for him. A generous treatment of properties and relations leads to the conclusion that it is also *complete!*

Suppose that we treat the properties and relations in the world as closed under truth-functions and projection (e.g. if *x is a parent of y* is a relation, *x is a parent* is a property; if *is happy* is a property and *is tall* is a property, *is happy and tall* is a property, etc.).[6] (However we feel about such generosity we should note that it creates no new *truths*, since the truths that we can state by reference to this enlarged class of predicates and relations we have already by supervenience.)[7]

Then Tractarian possible worlds with respect to second-order logic correspond to Henkin's *general models* of second order logic, rather to what logicians have called the '*natural*' models. The 'natural' models are only natural if we are nominalists in a rather different sense from the one being developed here. In the 'natural' models the property quantifiers are interpreted as ranging over *all* subsets of the objects of the world (and the relation quantifiers over *all* subsets of the appropriate cartesian product of the individual domain). In other words, properties and relations are taken as *parasitic* on objects. What properties and relations exist in a model depend on what objects do. In Tractarian Nominalism however, we regard the relational quantifiers as ranging over real physical relations whose existence is every bit as contingent as that of physical objects – and consequently the relations which exist in a world may only correspond to some subset of the 'natural' domain, and it is basically this fact which makes second order logic *complete* for the Tractarian Nominalist.

Since the Tractarian Nominalist recognizes only such higher order propositions as are supervenient on first order models, we cannot extend the argument to higher order logic. The natural logic for a Tractarian Nominalist is second-order quantification.

6 [Added by Skyrms for this volume: These closure conditions come from lambda abstraction in the version of higher-order logic considered by Henkin. Restricted closure conditions of the kind favored by Armstrong could be accommodated by corresponding restrictions on this principle.]
7 Note, in this connection, that there is no real need for negative facts, disjunctive facts, etc. in the semantics of tractarian nominalism since the propositions they are intended to service are supervenient on the first-order *atomic* facts. This points up the difference between Tractarian Nominalism as here presented, and the positions of Russell, Armstrong, and Bergmann.

It is clear by now that the metaphysics that I have been referring to by the provocative oxymoron 'Tractarian Nominalism' is neither wholly Tractarian nor wholly nominalistic, although it is in sympathy with strands of both lines of thought. It is perhaps closer to Russell's view in the second edition of *Principia Mathematica* than to the *Tractatus*.[8] (Russell, however, has no thesis of supervenience.) For it, I claim these virtues: First, it shifts our focus of attention from the metaphysics of the subject (or the individual variable) to the metaphysics of the whole assertion which is really 'where the action is'. That Matilda does the waltz, that Matilda waltzes, that Matilda dances waltzingly, that the waltz is danced by Matilda, etc. should not be thought of radically metaphysically different; they all come to much the same thing. The Tractarian Nominalist can say that we have here different ways of specifying the same fact, even though the conception of the waltz has found accommodation in quite different parts of speech. Second, I claim that the traditional epistemological motivations for nominalism can be better taken as motivations for Tractarian Nominalism. This is almost a corollary to the first point, since our epistemological concern is primarily with *knowledge of truths* rather than with acquaintance with the denotata of subject terms or individual variables. Third, I claim that the view helps us to think in a level-headed way about possibilities and possible worlds. In particular, it helps us distinguish stages in the construction of possibilia and it helps us to see at which stage haecciatism is appropriate and at which stage it is not. Fourth, Tractarian Nominalism gives a metaphysical foundation for second order logic. This comes from treating properties and relations as contingent existents on a par with individuals. Both are ontologically parasitic on, and epistemologically prior to, facts. Both are investigated by empirical science. The criteria of individuation of physical properties in a science at a time may not always be crystal clear, but neither are the criteria of individuation for physical objects. (It is easier to distinguish the property of being-an-electron from the property of being-a-proton, than to distinguish the electrons from each other!) Given a generous attitude toward

8 Compare Russell, Putnam, and Armstrong.

closure of properties and relations under truth functions and projections, Tractarian Nominalism supplies a natural reading on which standard second-order logic is not only sound, but also complete.

I think that Tractarian Nominalism is a live metaphysical option, and an attractive one.[9]

BIBLIOGRAPHY

Armstrong, D. M.: *Universals and Scientific Realism* (2 vols.) (Cambridge University Press, Cambridge, 1978).

Bergmann, G.: 'Elementarism', *Philosophy and Phenomological Research* 18 (1957), pp. 107–114, reprinted in: *Meaning and Existence* (University of Wisconsin Press, Madison, 1968), pp. 115–123.

Goodman, N.: 'A world of individuals', in: *The Problem of Universals* (Notre Dame University Press, Notre Dame, Indiana, 1956).

Goodman, N. and W. V. O. Quine: 'Steps toward a constructive nominalism', *Journal of Symbolic Logic* 12 (1947), pp. 97–122.

Henkin, L.: 'Completeness in the theory of types', *Journal of Symbolic Logic* 15 (1956), pp. 89–91.

Kaplan, D.: 'How to Russell a Frege–Church' (*sic*), *Journal of Philosophy* 72 (1975), pp. 716–729.

Putnam, H.: 'On properties', in: *Essays in Honor of Carl G. Hempel*, ed. by Rescher et al. (D. Reidel, Dordrecht, Holland, 1970); reprinted in H. Putnam, *Mathematics, Matter and Method* (Cambridge University Press, Cambridge, 1975).

Quine, W. V. O.: 'On what there is', in: *From a Logical Point of View*, 2nd rev. ed. (Harper, New York and Evanston, 1961), pp. 1–19.

Quine, W. V. O.: 'Whither physical objects', *Boston Studies in the Philosophy of Science*, Vol. 39 (D. Reidel, Dordrecht, 1976), pp. 497–504.

Russell, B. and A. N. Whitehead: *Principia Mathematica*, 2nd ed. (Cambridge University Press, Cambridge, 1927), especially the preface to the second edition and Appendix C.

9 I would like to thank David Armstrong, Alan Code, Ed Gettier, Leslie Tharp, and Kent Wilson for helpful comments on an earlier version of this paper. [Added by Skyrms for this volume: Although I develop Tractarian Nominalism here in an atomistic framework, I agree with Armstrong that it is possible and desirable to pursue the basic idea in a more general setting where the existence of logical atoms is not presupposed.]

Index

153

156

For EU product safety concerns, contact us at Calle de José Abascal, 56–1°,
28003 Madrid, Spain or eugpsr@cambridge.org.

www.ingramcontent.com/pod-product-compliance
Ingram Content Group UK Ltd.
Pitfield, Milton Keynes, MK11 3LW, UK
UKHW012341130625
459647UK00009B/440